Aliens and Others

Aliens and Others

Science Fiction, Feminism and Postmodernism

Jenny Wolmark

University of Iowa Press, Iowa City

Copyright © 1994 by Jenny Wolmark

All rights reserved

University of Iowa Press, Iowa City 52242

International Standard Book Numbers 0-87745-446-9 cloth,
0-87745-447-7 paper

Library of Congress Catalog Card Number 93-60971
98 97 96 95 94 C 5 4 3 2 1
98 97 96 95 94 P 5 4 3 2 1

Printed in Great Britain

To Geoff and Nick
and to my mother Kathleen

Contents

Preface

There has been an increase in both general and academic interest in the science fiction (SF) genre in the last few years, and this parallels other cultural developments, such as the acknowledged overlap between postmodern fiction and SF, and the production of a range of films which are situated loosely within SF but which cross over into other genres, particularly that of horror.

In SF itself, distinctions of all kinds have always been blurred. Those who read SF often end up writing it, or writing about it, or both. In addition, fandom in SF has produced a range of informed and often innovative publications that deserve serious attention. Feminist science fiction participates fully on all these different terrains, and its participation has been crucial to the development of the genre, despite the fact that it has often had to argue vociferously for its concerns to be taken seriously.

This book is intended as a contribution to that on-going argument. I have drawn on a range of theoretical positions from within feminist theory, literary theory and cultural theory, to examine texts that in themselves are determinedly boundary crossing. Although it is primarily academic in its address, the blurring of boundaries between the consumer, the practitioner and the academic means that this address cannot, and indeed should not, be regarded as an exclusionary device.

My own position as a feminist, an academic and an avid reader of science fiction reflects this propensity to negotiate boundaries, and I have derived great satisfaction from that sense of being able to move between positions and identities. I recommend the experience, and hope that readers, both of this book and of the novels that I have chosen to discuss, will be open to a similar process of negotiation.

Acknowledgements

I owe a large debt of thanks to the friends and colleagues with whom I work in Theoretical Studies for providing me with the time and opportunity to complete this book.

I am grateful to my editor Jackie Jones, both for her invaluable advice on the manuscript and her general reassurance in moments of panic.

I am also grateful to Sarah Lefanu for her comments on the manuscript, and if I have not been able to incorporate all of them here, I intend to do so elsewhere.

A Note About Editions

It will be noticed that book titles quoted in the text are sometimes followed by two publication dates. Where two dates have been included in the same bracket, the first is the original date of publication, the second is the date of the actual edition from which I have quoted in the text. The reason for this arrangement is that, owing to the vagaries of paperback publishing, there is often a considerable gap in time between the American and British publication of the same book, and not all American titles are reprinted by British publishers.

Chapter 1

Intersections

Introduction

Although the main focus of this study is feminist science fiction, it is clear that in recent years science fiction as a whole has been increasingly identified with such postmodernist concerns as the instability of social and cultural categories, the erosion of confidence in historical narratives and a seemingly concomitant inability to imagine the future. Familiar science fiction metaphors exploring the interface between human and machine, depicting the other as alien, or dislocating spatial and temporal relations appear frequently in postmodern narratives. The extension of communications technology into every aspect of social and cultural life is no longer an imagined or science fictional future; it has already taken place, with consequences that are both alarming and hopeful. As the distinction between the imaginary and the real, and the present and the future, becomes less obvious, the generalised definition of science fiction as a popular genre in which utopian or dystopian fantasies of the future are explored clearly requires further consideration.

It is not only the thematic and linguistic convergence of science fiction and postmodernism which suggests that such a reconsideration is appropriate, however. An equally significant convergence between feminism and science fiction since the 1970s has resulted in the production of texts in which gender and identity are central, as is the depiction of new and different sets of social and sexual relations. Feminist science fiction has brought the politics of feminism into a genre with a solid tradition of ignoring or excluding

1

women writers, and in so doing it has politicised our understanding of the fantasies of science fiction. To do so, it has drawn on feminist analysis of the construction of gendered subjectivity in order to suggest possibilities for more plural and heterogeneous social relations, and to offer a powerful critique of the way in which existing social relations and power structures continue to marginalise women.

The emphasis on gender and difference, in conjunction with the postmodern erosion of boundaries between high and popular culture, has had unsettling consequences for the genre, which, somewhat unexpectedly, has become a terrain for the ideological contestation of the politics of gender. Donna Haraway's definition of SF usefully describes the way in which the genre has incorporated these concerns: 'Science fiction is generically concerned with the interpenetration of boundaries between problematic selves and unexpected others and with the exploration of possible worlds in a context structured by transnational technoscience.'[1] The way in which the 'problematic selves and unexpected others' within feminist science fiction challenge the fixed relations of gender, and of self and other, and insist on exploring other representational possibilities, is the subject of this book.

The book is, then, primarily a study of the ways in which feminist science fiction addresses questions of subjectivity, identity and difference, and challenges the dual definition of the 'alien' as other and of the other as always being alien. Science fiction provides a rich source of generic metaphors for the depiction of otherness, and the 'alien' is one of the most familiar: it enables difference to be constructed in terms of binary oppositions which reinforce relations of dominance and subordination. Since feminist science fiction occupies a marginal position in relation to other forms of cultural production, it is well placed to invest this and other metaphors with new and different meanings which undermine ostensibly clear-cut distinctions between self and other, human and alien. It explores possibilities for alternative and non-hierarchical definitions of gender and identity within which the difference of aliens and others can be accommodated rather than repressed.

The context for this study is provided by the intersections between feminism, postmodernism and science fiction, which are the subject of the introductory chapter. Although they are always problematic and often inconclusive, such intersections nevertheless have the capacity to draw our attention to the need constantly to redefine positions and meanings, in order to include what has previously been excluded, and to recognise that new forms of social and cultural experience require new forms of response. The use of the term 'intersections' is intended to suggest those cross-over points where discourses become openly contradictory, and boundaries become flexible and subject to renegotiation. Feminist science fiction exists at just such a point of intersection, or intertextuality, where the paradoxical conditions of its own existence enable the production of texts that address new and different issues and audiences: its feminist intentions mean that it functions disruptively within a masculinist popular genre, the generic outlines of which are already in the process of redefinition as the boundaries between high and popular culture become increasingly insecure.

The texts that are discussed in subsequent chapters demonstrate the varied and often contradictory ways in which contemporary feminist science fiction has responded to the unstable terrain of cultural and gender politics. Despite their differences, there is still a sense of a shared agenda in these texts, since they are all concerned in some way with redefining the female subject outside the confines of the binary oppositions that seek to fix gender identities in the interests of existing relations of domination. The marginalised others of race and gender are central to the novels of Octavia Butler and Gwyneth Jones, and the discussion of their work in Chapter 2 focuses on the way in which the texts use the device of the alien to explore otherness. The reworking of the opposition between human and alien in Butler's work recalls the narratives of slavery, and the power relations inherent in those narratives remain a disturbing feature of the novels that are discussed here. Gwyneth Jones' novel is a complex and profoundly ironic study of the contradictions inherent in science fiction narratives when the alien becomes the expression of a culture's simultaneous fear of and desire for the other. This eminently postmodern narrative reflexively traces the way in which the generic device of the alien has been used to displace difference into the realms of the transcendental, so that the material implications of marginalisation and difference continue to go unrecognised. As an alien contact narrative, the text is therefore concerned with the conditions of its own existence as much as it is with the meanings attached to the device of the alien. Definitions of otherness thus become impossible to sustain as the question of who is 'alien' becomes increasingly unanswerable, particularly from within science fiction narratives themselves.

Chapter 3 examines the way in which the generic conventions and narrative strategies of science fiction are subverted within the novels of C.J. Cherryh and Vonda McIntyre, as are the gendered and unequal power structures and social relations embedded within them. Both writers disrupt the definitions of otherness that are sustained by those conventions and strategies, particularly by the opposition between nature and culture, and in so doing produce narratives that are both contradictory and open-ended. Although some of the novels by C.J. Cherryh that are discussed in this chapter are peopled by generically familiar aliens, she also uses the notion of the genetically engineered human, who is therefore both alien and other, to problematise the distinction between human and non-human, self and other. Vonda McIntyre considers the way in which the interface between human and machine destabilises definitions of gender and identity, thus undermining the opposition between self and other. The 'cyborg monsters' of McIntyre's novels in particular are concerned to re-present gender outside the confines of fixed subject positions, so that other possibilites for social and sexual relations can be explored.

The social and political gains that women made in the 1970s, which have been significantly eroded throughout the 1980s, have found expression in the post-apocalyptic scenarios of feminist science fiction that are the subject of Chapter 4. The confidently depicted separatist utopias of the 1970s, such as those by Suzy McKee Charnas and Sally Miller Gearhart, contained many ambiguities about gender relations, and this has become increasingly obvious as more recent versions of women-only communities confront the essentialist nature of those utopias. The distinction between utopia and dystopia becomes less clear in the communities created by Sheri Tepper, Pamela Sargent, and Margaret Atwood, each of which refer to enclosure and liminality in a way that the earlier novels did not. The argument in this chapter suggests that the unresolvable contradictions that arise from this liminality reflect the writers' concern with gendered subjectivity and with redefining the limits of the self.

The final chapter is concerned with the impact of cyberpunk on feminist science fiction, particularly in the light of the often remarked upon absence of any real engagement with technology in feminist science fiction. Cyberpunk has its own absences, however, one of which is the unacknowledged influence of feminist SF, and cyberpunk narratives are marked by anxieties about gender relations. This aspect of cyberpunk is discussed in relation to the work of William Gibson, whose writing is most clearly identified with the emergence of cyberpunk and the new spatial metaphor of 'cyberspace'. The main argument put forward in this chapter is that, despite the male ethos of cyberpunk and its largely uncritical celebration of the mysteries of the human–machine interface, its active engagment with technology and its oppositional qualities are of considerable relevance to writers of feminist SF, as the work of the writers discussed in the chapter demonstrates. Pat Cadigan, one of the few women writing in the cyberpunk idiom, is concerned to demystify the human–machine interface so that the new conceptual space opened up by cyberpunk can be used to reconsider gender and identity. The erosion of boundaries between the real and the simulated that is suggested by 'cyberspace' enables both Cadigan and Rebecca Ore to use this metaphor of cybernetic systems to explore questions of gender and identity, self and other.

The work of Marge Piercy and Elisabeth Vonarburg is more obliquely inflected towards the human–machine interface: a key metaphor for these writers is the cyborg, whose radical possibilities for gender and identity have been identified by Donna Haraway. She describes the cyborg as 'a fiction mapping our social and bodily reality and as an imaginative resource suggesting some very fruitful couplings'.[2] In the work of Piercy and Vonarburg, the human–machine interface becomes the site at which the oppositional relations between self and other can be reconfigured, so that difference can be seen to make a significant contribution towards the constitution of new kinds of subjects and subject relations.

Intersections

The central argument in the book is that the aliens and others of feminist science fiction are explored within a framework that is increasingly informed by both feminist theory and postmodernism. Before any detailed discussion of specific texts can take place, it will be necessary, therefore, to provide an overview of the determining

characteristics of postmodernism and feminism, and of the intersections between them and the genre as a whole. The development
of science fiction, from its origins in nineteenth-century gothic
literature to the present day, has been more than adequately covered
by other writers,[3] and since it is not the particular concern of this
study, that knowledge has been largely taken for granted.

Science Fiction and Postmodernism

Postmodernism has been described by Andreas Huyssen as existing
in a 'field of tension between tradition and innovation, conservation
and renewal, mass culture and high art, in which the second terms
are no longer automatically privileged over the first'.[4] Huyssen is
describing the implicit hierarchy of values within a set of cultural
dominants that has operated to marginalise the products of popular
culture, but which is becoming increasingly unstable. As generic outlines become blurred within postmodernism, the positioning of texts
within high and popular culture has become uncertain, as the interaction between science fiction and postmodern fiction demonstrates.

While such interaction is recognised as taking place, its
disruptive potential is not always given a similar recognition. This
is the case in Brian McHale's *Postmodernist Fiction* (1987) which is
otherwise open in its acknowledgement of the interplay between
science fiction and postmodern fiction:

> There is, then, ample evidence of postmodernist writing's indebted-
> ness to the science fiction genre. But the indebtedness also runs in the
> opposite direction. Just as postmodernism has borrowed ontological
> motifs from science fiction, so science fiction has in recent years begun
> to borrow from postmodernism.[5]

Despite the two-way traffic between science fiction and postmodernism, McHale is nevertheless at great pains to describe the
relationship between them in terms of an advance along 'parallel
literary–historical tracks', whereby each has 'been pursuing analog-
ous but independent courses of development'.[6] What is acknowledged as a fruitful exchange of motifs and *topoi* is not, then,
considered sufficient to constitute a significant breakdown of the
boundaries between high and popular culture, and all that has
happened is that those boundaries have been slightly re-adjusted.

While postmodernist fiction may have a self-consciousness about its use of contradictory and competing discourses, its essentially 'literary' characteristics remain unchanged in McHale's view, just as its essential concerns continue to be issues of alienation and selfhood, refashioned in postmodernist style. Redefinition of these issues to take account of feminist deconstructions of the subject, for example, does not occur in McHale's account, any more than does a reconsideration of the relations between science fiction and postmodernist fiction, or of the meaning of the 'literary' itself.

A description of postmodernism that does take account of the possibilities inherent in postmodern intersections of the kind that are being suggested in this study is provided by Peter Brooker: he suggests that postmodernism is a 'shift, prompted and enabled by social, economic and technological change, into the heteroglossia of inter-cultural exchange, as idioms, discourse across the arts and academy, and across these and popular or mass forms, are montaged, blended or blurred together'.[7] The notion of 'inter-cultural exchange' is a useful way of thinking about postmodern intersections: it recognises the complex effects of such exchanges whilst maintaining the specificity of the sites from which such exchanges are initiated. Thus the intersections between science fiction, feminism and postmodernism that are discussed in this study do not produce a decentred and formless amalgam of discourses, nor do they result in the conflation of one site into the other(s), rather they produce new and challenging perspectives on each of those sites. In the context of his discussion of postmodernism and SF, Roger Luckhurst makes a comment that can be applied equally well to each of the areas under consideration here: 'The specificity of SF, its forms, temporality, and modes of enunciation, must be retained in order to say anything meaningful about it.'[8] If postmodern fiction and science fiction are not to be conflated, then neither are feminism and postmodernism, a point that is made later in the chapter.

In the sections that follow, postmodernism will be discussed in terms of Fredric Jameson's influential formulation of it as the 'cultural dominant' of late capitalism, and of Jean Baudrillard's emphasis on the displacement of the real by the simulacra. Both Jameson and Baudrillard are concerned with the way in which changes in the social and political spheres are increasingly expressed in terms of the cultural, so that, in a thoroughly commodified cultural environment, the ability to make meaningful interventions has been thrown into question. Both also use the generic specificity of science fiction as a source of metaphors on which to draw when defining the ever-shifting environment of postmodernism. Science fiction renders temporal relations uncertain and makes the familiar appear strange, and its fantasies of the future provide a critical view of the present. Jameson in particular has referred to the way in which science fiction 'enacts and enables a structurally unique "method" for apprehending the present as history'.[9] Since postmodernism is equally preoccupied with such concerns, it is perhaps not suprising to find parallels being drawn between them.

One of the major problems with which postmodernism confronts us is precisely that of definition, particularly since postmodern theory itself has argued for the collapse of the universal narratives which sustained critical theory. If contemporary socio-economic conditions can be described in terms of postmodernity and their corresponding cultural relations are described in terms of the postmodern, then postmodernism itself can be described as a historical condition, or, as David Harvey suggests, as a 'historical–geographical condition of a certain sort'.[10] Fredric Jameson also views postmodernism as a historical condition, seeing it from within the framework of Marxism as the 'cultural logic of late capitalism'. However, the attempt to provide some kind of historical specificity for postmodernism as a 'cultural dominant' is almost immediately undermined by the postmodern irony towards such unitary theoretical overviews. Since we are without recourse to grand narratives, and since we are situated, as Jameson says, 'within the culture of postmodernism',[11] theorisations of the postmodern become fraught with difficulty, appearing as both contradictory and self-referential.

The difficulty of finding an appropriately distanced and critical position from which to analyse the historical and cultural specificity of postmodernism does not, however, preclude the possibility that critical spaces can be negotiated and developed within the unresolved territory left by disintegrating critical and cultural boundaries and categories, in other words, at the intersections described earlier. While this approach does not obviate the difficulty of theorising the conditions of postmodernism and postmodern cultural production, it seeks to avoid the fixity of totalising theory by employing a decentred critical strategy in which boundaries are assumed to be flexible and subject to dissolution. The cultural pessimism expressed by Fredric Jameson in his essay 'Postmodernism and consumer society' (1985), however, appears to leave little room for the development of oppositional positions in relation to the dominant characteristics of the postmodern, in contrast to what he sees as the manifestly subversive intent of modernist cultural practice.

Jameson suggests that postmodernism is a generalised reaction to 'high' modernism and as such has no particular coherence, but is rather a series of elements which, when taken together, are expressive of the socio-enonomic conditions of late multinational capitalism. In the postmodern period, the works of high modernism have themselves been co-opted into academic institutions, and in the process have lost their subversive and critical intent. The commodification of culture, the invasive domination of information technology, the decentring and fragmentation of the individual and the blurring of boundaries between high and popular culture are part of a significant cultural shift which corresponds to the socio-enonomic changes of late capitalism. Jameson uses the term schizophrenia to describe what he sees as one of the most striking characteristics of that shift, which is the breakdown in the previously stable relationships between signifiers which produces a 'rubble of distinct and unrelated signifiers'.[12] Since understanding of the relationship between past, present and future, and of temporality generally, depends on the inter-relations between signifiers, once the chain of meaning is broken the schizophrenic subject is condemned to live in what Jameson describes as 'a perpetual present'. The schizophrenic present of postmodernism, in which signifiers are separated from their signifieds, can therefore be seen to mark the emergence of a new set of relations which are characterised by heterogeneity and discontinuity and dominated by the spatial rather than the temporal.

The most urgent feature of postmodern cultural relations is, then, the 'disappearance of a sense of history',[13] which produces a fascination with the 'hallucinatory splendor' of surfaces and a corresponding depthlessness. This depthlessness flattens out both history and experience and this is what finally erodes the relative autonomy of culture and with it the critical distance between culture and theory. It is the absence of this critical distance that is invoked by Jameson's use of the term schizophrenia, a use that is described by Jacqueline Rose as the 'psychic metaphorization of contemporary cultural and social space'.[14] It enables Jameson to make the sweeping generalisation that the implosive spatial and social relations of postmodernism have extended into the realms of both the psychic and the social, and that in so doing they have deferred the development of any radical opposition to it as a cultural dominant.

The view that potentially oppositional responses have been all but excluded in postmodernism stems from Jameson's assumption that the erosion of the boundaries between high and popular culture has defused the radical and subversive intent of modernist cultural production. This ignores the oppositional capacities of popular culture by seeing it as part of that 'perpetual present' in which a commodified culture has expanded into all other spheres of social and psychic life. The new historical reality which this represents requires an appropriately new form of 'cognitive mapping' for which it seems we are, as yet, unequipped. This negative view of popular culture can also be found in an earlier article by Jameson on science fiction utopias, considered as part of those collective fantasies about the past and the future that are the expression of a culture's 'political unconscious'. The article discusses the complex ways in which contemporary science fiction 'registers fantasies about the future', [15] which are in effect representations of the most intolerable apects of the present. The role of contemporary SF, then, is 'to demonstrate and to dramatise our incapacity to imagine the future',[16] and its failure to represent the future becomes the means by which we are enabled to contemplate 'our own absolute limits'.

Jameson's view of the negative capacities of science fiction is in marked contrast to his view of the radical capacities of modernism to be a 'Utopian compensation for increasing dehumanization on the level of daily life'.[17] Despite its relevance to a discussion of the postmodern condition, Jameson appears to regard SF as very much part of the 'increasing dehumanization' of life, rather than as a genre capable of making meaningful social and cultural interventions. This view fails to recognise the potential of science fiction to offer alternative and critical ways of imagining social and cultural reality, an aspect of the genre that has been favourably commented on by Teresa de Lauretis: 'The science fictional construction of a possible world, on the contrary, entails a conceptual reorganization of semantic space and therefore of material and social relations, and makes for an expanded cognitive horizon, an epic vision of our present social reality.'[18] The oppositional possibilities of science fiction lie in its capacity to contribute towards an 'expanded cognitive horizon', rather than simply to reflect the way in which such horizons have been closed down within postmodernism.

Jameson has been criticised for overemphasising the hegemonic capacities of postmodernism, and it is clear that his analysis fails to take account of the way in which new and contradictory social constituencies have emerged within postmodernity to challenge existing hierarchies and subjectivities. The formation of new subject positions in terms of race, gender and class, and redefinitions of identity as provisional and plural are an important and oppositional response to the disappearance of the unitary subject, and yet their capacity to forge new ways of conceptualising the link between history and subjectivity is consistently underestimated by Jameson. In his emphasis on the hegemonic nature of postmodernism, Jameson imposes a curiously unilinear and unitary logic on its contradictory and incoherent features, but it is those contradictions that remain crucial in the resistance to totalising theories. The erosion of the boundary between high art and popular culture results in the production of texts that are undoubtedly contradictory, but this does not negate their utopian and radical possibilities, and in the case of feminist science fiction, it is the imagining of these possibilities that is of particular importance.

Jameson's account of postmodernism is predicated on the assumption that since the modernist aesthetic tradition is 'dead', all that can follow is empty repetition. The erosion of cultural boundaries and the development of new forms of cultural production, such as feminist science fiction, are therefore considered to be equally empty. However, the decentring of the modernist legacy, along with the decentring of the unitary subject, have been of immense importance as far as feminism and feminist cultural production is concerned, enabling the question of gendered subjectivity to become part of the postmodern agenda. The social and cultural significance of these developments is discounted as Jameson formulates the problem of gender and identity in purely aesthetic terms:

> What we have to retain from all this is rather an aesthetic dilemma: because if the experience and the ideology of the unique self, an experience and ideology which informed the stylistic practice of classical modernism, is over and done with, then it is no longer clear what the artists and writers of the present period are supposed to be doing.[19]

Although feminist artists and writers, including those who write science fiction, have been very clear about the necessity to theorise their practice in relation to both modernism and postmodernism, Jameson takes little account of these views.

The collapse of the distinctions between past, present and future and between the real and the simulated are also central to Baudrillard's conceptualisation of the postmodern, and, like Jameson, Baudrillard also uses science fiction as a reference point. For both Jameson and Baudrillard, the influence of communications technology and the postmodern fascination with surfaces are seen as crucial influences in the shift in values that marks postmodernism, described by Baudrillard as the 'era of simulation': 'All the great humanist criteria of value, all the values of a civilization of moral, aesthetic, and practical judgment, vanish in our system of images and signs. Everything becomes undecidable.'[20] Just as Jameson notes the loss of 'critical distance' in postmodernism, so Baudrillard comments on the disappearance of the critical contradiction between the real and the imaginary, in a world which 'has become a collective marketplace not only for products but also for values, signs, and models, thereby leaving no room any more for the imaginary'.[21]

As relations of consumption have replaced those of production, so simulation has replaced the critical connections between theory and practice, the real and the imaginary, and as a result all signs and values have become non-referential, indeterminate and free floating:

> At this level, the question of signs and their rational destination; their *real* and their *imaginary*; their repression; their reversal; the illusions they sketch; what they hush up, or their parallel significations – all of these are swept from the table.[22]

In a world of indeterminacy and hyper-reality, signs are freed from their relations with the real, and signs of the real are substituted for the real itself. Baudrillard's self-referential 'desert of the real' is a place in which the real exists only in an 'hallucinatory resemblance to itself', as simulation.[23] Similarly, the relationship between reality and illusion can no longer be maintained, since the reality on which the illusory was based no longer exists. His analysis of the media in particular suggests that the boundaries between the real and the simulated are imploding, so that the hyper-real has become not a parody of the real, but more real than the real itself.

Baudrillard takes Disneyland as an example of the hyper-real, and rather than treating it as an ideological account of the imaginary resolution of the unresolvable contradictions of American life, he suggests that 'Disneyland is presented as imaginary in order to make us believe that the rest is real.'[24] In other words, the boundary between Disneyland and the 'real' America has dissolved, and the real has been replaced by simulation and the hyper-real. The hyper-real means 'the end of metaphysics, the end of fantasy, the end of SF'.[25] It is not entirely clear what version of the 'real' has been negated by the hyper-real, but Baudrillard's nostalgic lament for the disappearance of 'all the great humanist criteria of value' is reminiscent of Jameson's regret at the passing of the modernist aesthetic.

In the larger scale of things, Baudrillard suggests that history, too, has 'ceased to exist', and has become an unsustainable and implosive narrative, in common with the social and the political. In 'The year 2000 has already happened', he describes the 'end' and the 'disappearance' of history, and the implosion of the future into the science fictional nature of the present:

> It is thus not necessary to write science fiction: we have as of now, here and now, in our societies, with the media, the computers, the circuits, the networks, the acceleration of particles which has definitively broken the referential orbit of things.[26]

In positing both the end of history and the absence of the future, Baudrillard appears to have abandoned the realms of the social and of the political. In the entropic era of simulation, the only oppositional response that is possible takes the form of silence and inertia on the part of the masses in the face of constant media 'noise' and excess information: this refusal to act or to respond constitutes, paradoxically, a political act carried out by those who are no longer subjects but who have been reconstituted as objects.

The highly abstract and metaphorical content of these formulations inevitably detracts from Baudrillard's often insightful analysis of the social and cultural dislocations that constitute the experience of postmodernity. By presenting simulation and the hyper-real as the dominant characteristics of the postmodern, Baudrillard has been able to account for the commodification of culture and the corresponding expansion of the cultural into the realms of the social, the economic and the political. Where Jameson's analysis of postmodernism continues to adhere to a theoretical framework in which a Marxist analysis of capital and class relations has central significance, Baudrillard has instead evoked a curious totalitarianism of the hyper-real in which all forms of social life are reduced to simulacra, and all distinctions between the private and public, inner and outer, subject and object have become impossible to sustain. At the same time, however, Baudrillard's allegorical narratives are nostalgic for these former categories, even while they are documenting their breakdown.

In a useful overview of the development of Baudrillard's ideas, Best and Kellner suggest that his work should be read as a 'science fiction fantasy of a potential future',[27] rather than as social theory. Baudrillard's work has certainly been influenced by science fiction writers such as J.G. Ballard, and this description is helpful for indicating the extent to which Baudrillard's analysis of postmodernism has become increasingly ironic and metaphorical. In the essay 'Simulacra and science fiction' (1991), Baudrillard draws explicitly on science fiction to illustrate once again the profoundly negative consequences of the postmodern collapse of the distinction between the real and the simulated. He argues that 'classic SF' was a fiction of 'expanding universes' which can no longer be sustained in a system which is reaching its limits in terms of globalisation, media saturation and simulation. In a situation in which it is no longer possible to create the imaginary from the details of the real, SF has become implosive, striving to 'reinvent the real as fiction, precisely because the real has disappeared from our lives'. Science fiction, then, can only concern itself with reproducing an 'hallucination of the real', since it can no longer be 'a mirror held to the future'. Increasingly, as the borders between science fiction and the real are eroded, it becomes the task of contemporary SF to present us with the fiction that is our own world, in a final demonstration that 'The simulation is impassable, unsurpassable, *checkmated*, without exteriority.'[28]

Just as Jameson defined science fiction as an indicator of our failure to imagine the future, so Baudrillard suggests that, since 'we can no longer imagine other universes', then SF can only operate repetitively within the hyper-real to 'revitalize, to reactualize, to rebanalize fragments of simulation – fragments of this universal stimulation which our presumed "real" world has now become for us'.[29] The conditions of existence of contemporary science fiction are also those of postmodernism: where once it was the role of SF to imagine fantasies of the future which confirmed the relation between the real and the imaginary, that role has been negated by the derealisation of the real. The task of science fiction, which is also the task of theory, is to re-invent the real as fiction, from within the hyper-real. Ideological contestation within postmodernism is thus inevitably forestalled by the circular relationship between the real and the simulated. The nature of the 'real' that would emerge from the 'revitalisation' of fragments of the simulated is, therefore, unclear, and the question of whose interests would be represented in it – and, indeed, *who* would be represented in it – is not asked. What does seem clear, however, is that as the specificity of human experience is displaced by simulation, then the lived realities of oppression and subordination experienced by women have no way of being expressed. Women remain outside the realms of language and of social signification even as the real is replaced by the simulated. The absolutely central questions of representation and of the historical and cultural construction of gendered subjectivity evidently do not get on the agenda in any re-invention of the 'real'.

Both Baudrillard and Jameson appropriate the science fictional, rather than the literary or philosophical, metaphor of utopia in order to demonstrate the way in which its progressive characteristics, which must include the possibility of imagining other ways of being, have been reversed by the dissolution of the boundaries between high and popular culture, utopia and dystopia, in postmodernism. By situating it within science fiction, the idea of utopia can be given a suitably ironic and postmodernist inflection, so that it becomes a vehicle for nostalgia, a place in which the future can no longer be imagined, functioning as the repository of the real which can never be realised. The totalising perspective which this particular intersection between science fiction and postmodernism has produced is unable to take account of the different ways in which postmodernism has opened up new cultural spaces within which radically different forms of social and sexual relations can be imagined, such as those offered within feminist SF. It is simply not enough to think of these significant conceptual reorganisations in terms of the circularity of 're-invention', or pastiche, since they are operating within the far more dynamic field of what Fred Pfeil calls

> an epochal paradigm shift separating the progressive social thought and imaginary of the 1980s from that of the 1960s, and from Enlightenment- and organicist-driven thought and struggle *tout court*:

a struggle whose enabling conditions and energies are largely derived from the interaction of the new forces and relations of production we call 'post industrial' with the new non-essentialist, post-Enlightenment visions, practices, projects and energies which have come to us primarily out of contemporary feminism.[30]

Feminism and Postmodernism

The aporias that occur in accounts of the interaction between science fiction and postmodernism, which ignore both their gender inscriptions and the possibility of different forms of relations developing between them, are a consequence of the modernist fear that the invasive products of popular culture would devalue the products of high art. As Andreas Huyssen suggests, this fear enables mass culture to be conceptualised as 'the homogeneously sinister background on which the achievements of modernism can shine their glory'.[31] More significantly, Huyssen also argues that the distinction between high and popular culture, although it is rendered in aesthetic terms, is in fact a gendered distinction. The privileged realms of authenticity and high art are reserved for the masculine, whereas the popular and the everyday, which is the concern of mass culture, has been duly feminised by being considered in terms of the inauthentic and trivial, and, in historical terms, it therefore became modernism's 'other'. Despite the transformations of postmodernism, elements of this anxiety continue to inform accounts of the postmodern, including those already discussed. The failure to acknowledge the possibilities inherent in the exchanges between high and popular culture, particularly where women producers and performers are concerned, can therefore be situated within the gendered anxieties about the dissolution of boundaries. It is, therefore, appropriate to consider feminist science fiction in the light of the intersections between feminism and postmodernism, and these intersections are discussed in the following section.

In her account of postmodernism, Linda Hutcheon is careful to distinguish between postmodernism and feminism, suggesting that while postmodern texts are doubly coded as 'both complicitous with and contesting of the cultural dominants within which it operates',[32] the critical trajectory of feminism is oppositional, not complicitous. Attempts to conflate feminism and postmodernism by suggesting that feminism is a product of postmodern theory therefore misunderstand the combative edge to feminist deconstructions of the self. It was, after all, necessary for feminists to point out the absence of gender in postmodern accounts of the decentred and fragmented subject. While there are common concerns in both feminist and postmodern accounts of subjectivity, identity and difference, this should not lead to a position in which one set of discourses can therefore be assumed to 'account' for the other, as happens in Craig Owens' suggestion that 'women's insistence on difference and incommensurability may not only be compatible with, but also an instance of postmodern thought.'[33] The suggestion is made within a discussion in which he acknowledges 'a blind spot in our discussions of postmodernism in general: our failure to address the issue of sexual difference – not only in the objects we discuss, but in our own enunciation as well.'[34]

The description of feminism as 'an instance of postmodern thought' is just such an example of the gendered 'enunciation' which Owens claims to be aware of, and stems from his assumption that 'few women have engaged in the modernism/postmodernism debate.'[35] This assumption is challenged by Meaghan Morris's account of the numbers of women who have, in fact, been involved in discussions about postmodernism, but whose contributions have gone either unacknowledged or unrecognised in what she calls 'the myth of a postmodernism still waiting for its women'.[36] In opposition to the suggestion that postmodernism has been an enabling environment for feminism, Morris emphasises the way in which feminism 'has acted as one of the enabling conditions of discourse *about* postmodernism', which makes it 'appropriate to use feminist work to frame discussions of postmodernism, and not the other way around'.[37]

Certainly, not all feminist writers are convinced of the value of postmodern theory. Christine Di Stefano is particularly critical of 'the postmodern call to give up the privileging of gender',[38] arguing that the postmodern emphasis on multiplicity and diversity results in a disabling pluralism in which the female subject is dissolved into a multiplicity of other differences. She suggests that postmodernist theories of difference cannot account for the way in which gender continues to be deeply embedded in social and cultural structures, which is why it remains central to feminist analysis. Indeed, it is the more complex questions of gender relations and the ways in which the gendered subject is reconstituted in social and cultural terms, within specific historical locations, that are often ignored in postmodern theory. The many points of connection between postmodern and feminist critiques of representation and the construction of the subject should not obscure the possibility that deconstructions of the subject can lead to an effacement of the particular and specific oppressions experienced by women.

Sabina Lovibond is equally critical of postmodernism and the way in which postmodern theory undermines the rationalist and humanist agenda of the Enlightenment, in which is enshrined the notion of equality that provides the political impetus for social change, without proposing alternative mechanisms for change. She argues that without such a philosophical framework, postmodernism not only undermines the possibilities for radical social change but also negates the capacity of feminism to make political interventions:

> So postmodernism seems to face a dilemma: either it can concede the necessity, in terms of the aims of feminism, of 'turning the world upside down' in the way just outlined – thereby opening a door once again to the Enlightenment idea of a *total* reconstruction of society on rational lines; or it can dogmatically reaffirm the arguments already marshalled against that idea – thereby licensing the cynical thought that, here as elsewhere, 'who will do what to whom under the new pluralism is depressingly predictable'.[39]

While Lovibond's emphasis on the need for a strategy for political intervention is timely and appropriate, she has resorted to a restatement of the totalising theoretical framework of the Enlightenment and its inherent dualisms, in order to pose the either/or dilemma she describes. However, it is precisely that totalising framework and its exclusionary binarisms that are interrogated in postmodernism, and Lovibond is in danger of replicating them, albeit in the interests of feminism.

The identification of feminism with the goals and ideals of the Enlightenment rests on the notion that postmodernism represents a complete break from those goals and ideals and is therefore antithetical to feminism. However, as Sandra Harding has pointed out, a feminist postmodernism is inevitably implicated in the inheritance of the Enlightenment project, since the goal of social progress, defined from a feminist point of view, is at the heart of feminist theory, and it is, therefore, 'misleading to assume that the

line between feminist supporters and critics of Enlightenment
assumptions is as broadly drawn as many take it to be . . .'[40] Since
the goal of social progress in both Enlightenment and postmodernist
terms remains incomplete, Harding suggests that feminists can draw
on both sets of positions in order to develop a feminist theory that
is provisional and incomplete, which refuses totalising categories,
and is, as a consequence, oppositional and progressive. Despite the
attractions of this argument, the reasons for assuming that a
progressive politics of 'feminist solidarity' would necessarily emerge
from a position of 'permanent partiality' are unclear, as are the kinds
of theoretical developments or political interventions that could
result from such a position.

In contrast to Harding's view that the theoretical and political
fragmentation that results from an absence of grand narratives can
be viewed positively, Nancy Fraser and Linda J. Nicholson argue
that it is not necessary for feminism to abandon such narratives
altogether. They can still be useful in developing a theoretical
critique of patriarchal structures that is properly materialist, and
which addresses gender within other discourses that are socially and
culturally specific, such as 'class, race, ethnicity, age, and sexual
orientation'.[41] They take issue with the way in which Lyotard has
dismissed the 'grand narratives' of western culture such as 'the
dialectics of Spirit, the hermeneutics of meaning, the emancipation
of the rational or the working subject, or the creation of wealth'.[42]
Lyotard's scepticism is here directed towards the notion of progress
that is built into the grand narratives of the Enlightenment, of Hegel
and of Marxism. He argues that the fact that such a notion is no
longer sustainable indicates that there is a crisis of legitimation
within the 'grand recits' of modernity themselves, and that there is
'a sort of grief in the *Zeitgeist*' which means that 'It is no longer
possible to call development progress.'[43]

Fraser and Nicholson argue that the loss of confidence in and
legitimacy of the metanarratives is not necessarily beneficial to
feminism, precisely because it disallows any 'critique of broad-based
relations of dominance and subordination along lines like gender,
race, and class'.[44] They argue that it is possible for 'postmodern
feminism' to 'combine a postmodernist incredulity toward metanarratives with the social-critical power of feminism', and that it is
not necessary to 'abandon the large theoretical tools needed to
address large political problems'.[45] Despite the somewhat elusive

characterisation of this position as 'postmodern-feminist theory', it is nevertheless a politically enabling development which incorporates diversity and difference into feminist theory and politics, while maintaining the historical and cultural specificity of its analysis.

It moves a considerable way towards the kind of materialist politics outlined by Toril Moi, in which she draws on a three-tiered model of feminist struggle put forward by Julia Kristeva.[46] The first stage of this model consists of a feminism which is centred on the liberal struggle for equal rights for women; the second stage is a separatist feminism of difference which asserts that women are of value in themselves as women, rather than in terms of a patriarchal order which excludes them; the third stage is one in which all binary oppositions are deconstructed. As Moi suggests, it is impossible actually to separate the different stages, let alone opt for one at the expense of the others, since each is fully implicated in the other:

> Unlike Kristeva, however, I believe that feminists today have to hold all three positions simultaneously. Simply to take up Kristeva's 'third position' of deconstructed identities, as she herself advocates, is clearly impossible. For, if we live in metaphysical space, our necessary utopian wish to deconstruct sexual identities always runs up against the fact that patriarchy itself persists in oppressing women *as women*. We must, then, at once live out the contradictions of all three feminisms *and* agonistically take sides: simply sitting on the fence will never demolish patriarchy.[47]

As discussion of the previous writers has indicated, attempts to conflate postmodernism and feminism, or to suggest that feminism is a consequence of postmodern thought, depend on an analysis in which the material conditions of women's existence play no part, and in which their oppression, as women, goes unrecognised. Moi's position makes the politics of feminism, and all their necessary contradictions, visible. Since these contradictions prevent any easy accommodation between feminism and postmodernism, the intersection between them can be best be characterised as a 'shared theoretical moment',[48] in which more open-ended and provisional accounts of the subject and of social relations generally have emerged. Within both feminism and postmodernism, that provisionality will require the development of new forms of political struggle that are based around recognition of these new subjectivities and social constituencies.

Feminist Science Fiction

The intersection of feminism and science fiction has produced a similar emphasis on provisionality, in that it has resulted in the production of texts whose recognisable generic boundaries and continuities are consistently undermined by their subject matter, as Anne Cranny-Francis has indicated in her study of what she calls 'feminist genre fiction':

> Feminist theory and the experiential knowledge of women went into the making of feminist SF and the result was the remaking of a literary genre, a fundamental investigation of the conventions of that genre, both for their literary or narrative implications and for their embedded ideological significance(s).[49]

The 'investigation' of the genre has been informed by more than feminist theory and experiential knowledge, however, as has already been suggested: the intersections between science fiction and postmodernism, as well as those between feminism and postmodernism, and feminism and science fiction, have contributed to the complex accounts of gender and identity offered in feminist SF.

The fragmented and decentred narrative of Joanna Russ's *The Female Man* (1975; 1985) is a notable example of a text that explores the pleasures of dissonance and incongruity that occur when gender and genre are in conflict. Russ dispenses with the necessity for either a single plot or a specific time sequence by means of a narrative that shifts continuously between parallel universes, and between the four different female characters who inhabit them. Joanna, Janet, Jael and Jeannine are all aspects of 'Everywoman' but they are also stubbornly themselves: 'I said goodbye and went off with Laur, I, Janet; I also watched them go, I, Joanna; moreover I went off to show Jael the city, I, Jeannine, I Jael, I myself.

Goodbye, goodbye, goodbye.'[50]

Thus, they, and the narrative, remain fragmented, disrupting the familiar discursive practices of science fiction in a playful and witty way, and enabling Russ to explore the possibility suggested by Mary Gentile that women 'must begin to see themselves as in a network of multiple possibilities, multiple perspectives, multiple identities, where there is no clear split between "I" and "not-I", but rather a range or continuum of existence.'[51]

The instability of the genre is emphasised by the way in which feminist science fiction foregrounds female desire, and makes reference to other genres, particularly that of romance, in order to do so. Feminist SF challenges the way in which female desire is subordinated to the privileged position accorded to male desire within the genre, as Russ herself points out in a discussion of the work of one male SF writer, whose novel is 'one long proof that, for women, heterosexuality is so much physically pleasanter than lesbianism that it binds a woman not only to sexual pleasure but to one man in particular and to a whole ideology of male dominance'.[52] In opposition to this subordination of female desire, the narrative strategies of feminist SF have developed to 'provide women with possible scenarios for their own future development', as Pamela Sargent put it in the introduction to her pioneering collection of science fiction stories by women, *Women of Wonder*.[53] These strategies recognise what Joanna Russ calls 'the whole difficulty of science fiction, of genuine speculation: how to get away from traditional assumptions which are nothing more than traditional strait-jackets.'[54] Feminist SF is concerned with the complexities and ambiguities of contemporary definitions and representations of gender, and this concern places it within the terrain marked out by the contradictory relations between science fiction, feminism and postmodernism.

Although it is rare for feminist science fiction narratives to engage in narrative experimentation of the kind that is familiar in postmodern texts, they are nevertheless fully implicated in the complicitous and contradictory processes of postmodernism described by Hutcheon. Feminist science fiction is situated within a popular cultural genre which itself has an uneasy relationship with postmodernism, but it uses the mechanisms of the genre against it, in order to question the way in which science fiction narratives represent the gendered self. It utilises the genre's preoccupation with the future in order to suggest that the construction of subjectivity and identity is a process, and as such is always incomplete. As Stuart Hall says of cultural identity, it is 'a matter of "becoming" as well as being. It belongs to the future as well as to the past.'[55] The notion of a unified, integrated self is made as problematic in feminist science fiction as it is in more explicitly postmodern texts.

The territory of unresolved contradictions inhabited by postmodernism has been described in other terms by Samuel Delany,

who uses the term 'paraspace', as distinct from 'subspace', to define
the relations that exist between the narrative space of science fiction
and that of 'naturalistic' fiction. A paraspace does not exist

> in a hierarchical relation – at least not in a simple and easy hierarchical
> relation – to the narrative's 'real', or ordinary, space. What goes on
> in one subverts the other; what goes on in the other subverts the one.
> They change their weights all the time, throughout their stories. So
> calling it a subspace – with the prefix's strong suggestion of
> subordination – is wrong. A paraspace, or even an alternative space,
> with its much weaker – and more problematic – question of position
> and troubling supplementarity, is more to the point.[56]

The notion of paraspace also provides a useful way of thinking about
the way in which feminist science fiction exists within a gendered
space of 'troubling supplementarity'. It is a space in which
subjectivity and experience, gender and identity, can be re-imagined
in opposition to, and in recognition of, the dominant gendered
discourses.

The 'paraspace' within which feminist SF exists corresponds to
that 'elsewhere' described by Teresa de Lauretis, which consists in
'spaces in the margins of hegemonic discourses, social spaces carved
in the interstices of institutions and in the chinks and cracks of the
power–knowledge apparati'. De Lauretis uses the notion of an
'elsewhere' in a specific context, that of the need to 'theorize gender
beyond the limits of "sexual difference", and the constraints that
such a notion has come to impose on feminist critical thought'.[57] The
emphasis on sexual difference, and its limitations, are present in
Alice Jardine's discussion of the construction of the feminine in
Gynesis, in which she suggests that the rethinking provoked by the
crisis of legitimacy in the grand narratives of western culture has
opened up an 'elsewhere' or a space that is specifically coded as
feminine, because it

> has involved, above all, a reincorporation and a reconceptualization
> of that which has been the master narratives' own 'nonknowledge',
> what has eluded them, what has engulfed them. This other-than-
> themselves is almost always a 'space' of some kind (over which the
> narrative has lost control), and this space has been coded as *feminine*,
> as *woman*.[58]

Jardine argues that the feminine is both defined by and defines
the marginal spaces which emerge as the binary divisions of western

culture begin to collapse, and this marginalisation enables it to subvert the dominant masculinist cultural order. However, the radical potential of the marginal is undermined here by the way in which the feminine is equated with 'woman', and because the differences between women cannot be recognised in this equation, the female subject becomes a unified rather than a contradictory, and therefore multiple, subject. The female subject is thus defined solely by its marginality, rather than by, and in, the contradictory discourses of the dominant culture. In contrast, de Lauretis argues that it is gender, rather than the feminine, that is constructed in the social space that is 'elsewhere', and that the subject is therefore

> constituted in gender, to be sure, though not by sexual difference alone, but rather across languages and cultural representations; a subject en-gendered in the experiencing of race and class, as well as sexual, relations; a subject, therefore, not unified but rather multiple, and not so much divided as contradicted.[59]

The distinction discussed above, between the subject as gendered or as female, finds a parallel in the distinction that is made between 'feminine' writing and feminist writing, and all of these different positions become relevant when considering the nature of the cultural intervention that feminist SF is making. Although attempts to define feminine writing are problematic, its primary intention is to challenge and disrupt the dominant discourse by means of its experimental, fluid and non-linear qualities. In the work of Luce Irigaray and Hélène Cixous in particular, the practice of feminine writing is defined by the female body: feminine writing becomes the embodiment of woman and of female sexuality. Feminine texts are defined as oppositional because of the way in which they rupture the semantic and syntactical structures of the dominant culture; similarly, for Julia Kristeva, this means that women's writing is identified with the 'explosion of social codes: with revolutionary moments',[60] in other words, with the avant-garde.

However, these arguments are forced to ignore the existence of texts that are resolutely realist and conformist, but which are equally oppositional because they contain an explicit critique of the unequal power relations experienced by women within the dominant culture. Feminist science fiction can clearly be situated here: like feminism itself, it exists in a contradictory relationship to the hegemonic discourses to which it is opposed but on which it draws, and this is the reason for its oppositional capacity to open up new spaces for alternative representations of gender. It is because they are concerned with representations of gender that these spaces, conceived of in terms of an 'elsewhere' or a 'paraspace', cannot be coded as 'feminine' or as 'woman'. The texts that operate within these spaces can, however, be considered as feminist, because they destabilise and rupture the dominant ideology of gender by confronting the contradictions of gender representation, rather than assuming the existence of a unitary subject that is 'feminine' or 'masculine'.

Attempts are sometimes made to 'rescue' science fiction generally, and feminist SF in particular, from the marginal spaces that it occupies, and in which it reconfigures gender relations, so that its 'subversive potential' can be fully recognised. Marleen Barr argues that

> 'Feminist SF' – a term I once strongly advocated – has become inadequate and distorting. It is time to redefine feminist SF, to ensure that this literature's subversive potential is not nullified (and shunned by most Anglo-American feminist theorists) because of a generic classification connoting literary inferiority.[61]

In an extraordinary about-face, Barr has turned from being a vociferous advocate of the significance of the writing practices of feminist SF, to becoming an ardent supporter of a postmodern literary canon which has expanded to accommodate what she calls 'feminist fabulation'. Since this term includes what used to be known as feminist SF, it is clear that generic specificity has been abandoned in favour of 'an umbrella term for describing overlapping genres'; quite how knowledge of the way in which genres overlap is to be gained, when the genres themselves have been conceptually dissolved, is not clear. The claim that 'Reinventing the canon coincides with reinventing womanhood'[62] emphasises the essentially conservative nature of the position that Barr has adopted: the re-invention of the canon unquestioningly puts in place the same binary opposition of high and popular culture against which Barr insists she is arguing; in the same way, the re-invention of 'womanhood' places gender back into the context of the binarisms of fixed subject positions, against which feminist SF has been arguing.

The intersections that have been described, between science

fiction and postmodernism, feminism and postmodernism, and feminism and science fiction demand more than the re-introduction of familiar critical terms and territories. As has already been argued, such intersections are contradictory: they allow for movement between and across the boundaries of intersecting sites, creating a space within which genre, gender and identity can be redefined, and even while the specificity of those sites is recognised, so too are the changes taking place within them. Donna Haraway's use of the cyborg metaphor is particularly appropriate to a discussion of such contradictory encounters, since the cyborg is itself structured around contradictions which allow for 'transgressed boundaries, potent fusions, and dangerous possibilities'.[63] In the context of such transgressions, the unfixing of the seemingly stable categories of identity constructed around gender, race and class, becomes a means of contesting definitions of otherness, and in so doing, reconstituting subjectivity and identity in a non-totalising way.

The cyborg monsters of Haraway's imagination 'do not seek unitary identity', which is why cyborg imagery 'can suggest a way out of the maze of dualisms in which we have explained our bodies and our tools to ourselves'.[64] The cyborg is, then, an imaginative embodiment of the subject of feminism, described by de Lauretis as being 'at the same time inside *and* outside the ideology of gender, and conscious of being so, conscious of that twofold pull, of that division, that doubled vision'.[65] It is the way in which these necessary contradictions inform feminist science fiction that will be the subject of the following chapters.

Chapter 2

Unpredictable Aliens

To be different, or alien, is a significant if familiar cultural metaphor which marks the boundaries and limits of social identity. It allows difference to be marginalised and any dissonance to be smoothed away, thus confirming the dominance of the centre over the margins. As Jonathan Rutherford suggests:

> The centre invests the Other with its terrors. It is the threat of the dissolution of self that ignites the irrational hatred and hostility as the centre struggles to assert and secure its boundaries, that construct self from not-self.[1]

Those who are different are objectified and are denied the capacity to be active agents in the creation of their own subjectivity; in taking on a sense of their own otherness, they are disempowered. Octavia Butler and Gwyneth Jones, whose work is discussed in this chapter, use the science fiction metaphor of the alien to explore the way in which the deeply divisive dichotomies of race and gender are embedded in the repressive structures and relations of dominance and subordination. As feminist writers in a predominantly masculinist genre, they occupy a marginal position, but they work to subvert those structures and relations by the very act of exploring the experience of subordination.

The alien has often been used within science fiction to reproduce, rather than question, those divisions, as Ursula Le Guin has pointed out:

> If you deny any affinity with another person or kind of person, if you declare it to be wholly different from yourself – as men have done to

women, and class has done to class, and nation has done to nation –
you may hate it or deify it; but in either case you have denied its
spiritual equality and its human reality. You have made it into a thing,
to which the only possible relationship is a power relationship.[2]

In the work of Butler and Jones, the notion of being 'alien' carries
an alternative set of resonances: there is a sense of slippage between
sameness and difference, between centre and margins, so that the
boundaries blur and become indecisive. The limits of social and
cultural identity are tested when those who are different are depicted
as active subjects who resist both the hierarchical relation between
centre and margins and unitary definitions of difference. These
writers work to give the definition of the 'alien' other inflections than
those with which we are familiar, and in so doing they confront the
'terrors' of the centre and the way in which they are attributed to
the other.

Octavia Butler – The Alienated Others of Race and Gender

As a black feminist science fiction writer, Octavia Butler has made
it clear that she situates her writing in opposition to the way in which
both race and gender have been treated in science fiction, where the
alien has been used to represent Otherness:

> Science fiction has long treated people who might or might not exist
> – extraterrestrials. Unfortunately, however, many of the same science
> fiction writers who started us thinking about the possibility of
> extraterrestrial life did nothing to make us think about here-at-home
> variation – women, blacks, Indians, Asians, Hispanics, etc.[3]

The emphasis on difference in her fiction challenges the binary
oppositions of alien and non-alien, insider and outsider, masculine
and feminine. Butler is writing 'against the grain' in several senses,
as she has explained: 'Science fiction has always been nearly all
white, just as until recently, it's been nearly all male.'[4] Ruth
Salvaggio describes Butler's fiction as being 'stories of power:
enslavement and freedom, control and corruption, survival and
adjustment',[5] and the production and reproduction of relations of
power in terms of race and gender is at the core of Butler's writing.
Much of her fiction is concerned with strong, black female characters

who struggle against repressive power structures, and Butler has commented on her own position as a black feminist science fiction writer in those terms: 'I began writing about power because I had so little.'[6]

Her fiction is about identity and the dimensions of the 'other' within those relations of power, and she explores the possibilities that new forms of selfhood can emerge when existing relations of power are challenged by difference. Butler's fiction has consistently been concerned with transformations, difference, and the transgression of boundaries, which call into question the way in which the dominant discourses of race and gender attempt to fix definitions of 'alien' and 'other'. Sandra Y. Govan describes Butler's fiction as being generally concerned with the linked themes of 'Difference, adaptability, change and survival'[7] and Butler has emphasised the importance of these ideas to her fiction and to science fiction as a whole: 'This idea of change seems to me to be one of the biggest challenges I face as a writer – and the inability to face this is a big problem in a lot of SF. Some kind of important change is pretty much what SF is about.'[8] Her fiction is centrally concerned with the exploration of transitional states in which the boundaries between self and other become fluid, and in which the search for homogeneity is resisted. Although all of Butler's work contains allusions to and reworkings of slave narratives, discussion here will focus on the books in which those narratives are mediated through the science fiction device of the alien, specifically *Mind of my Mind* (1977; 1978), *Wild Seed* (1980), *Clay's Ark* (1985) and the three novels that make up the *Xenogenesis* trilogy, *Dawn* (1987; 1988), *Adulthood Rites* (1988; 1989), and *Imago* (1989; 1990).

In her most recent work, the *Xenogenesis* trilogy, Butler uses the device of the alien being to explore the cultural determinants of definitions of the other as a signifier of threat. The trilogy is set in a post-holocaust future in which the few remaining humans have been rescued from an uninhabitable Earth by an alien race called the Oankali. The Oankali are 'gene traders', that is, they combine their DNA molecules with the genetic material of whatever races they come into contact with so that each race is changed, in the Oankali view, for the better. In this way, races do not become fixed in their cultural categories and rigid in their modes of behaviour:

> We do what you would call genetic engineering. We know you had
> begun to do it yourselves a little, but it's foreign to you. We do it

naturally. We *must* do it. It renews us, enables us to survive as an evolving species instead of specializing ourselves into extinction or stagnation.[9]

The Oankali intend that a genetic exchange should take place between themselves and the humans that they have rescued from the annihilated earth, whether or not the remaining humans are willing. Although Butler poses the relationship between Oankali and humans in terms of mutually alien genetics and an equally mutual necessity for both species to change if they are to survive, the narrative is ambivalent towards the developing human–Oankali relations because it contains implicit echoes of the slave narrative. Butler not only poses some difficult questions about what it means to be human, but she also places those questions in the discomfiting context of the relations of subordination and domination within which both race and gender are situated.

In *Dawn*, the first novel of the trilogy, gender and race are central to the development of the narrative and are explored by means of Lilith's relationships both with the alien Oankali and with the other humans on the Oankali ship. Lilith Iyapo is a young black woman who has been chosen by the Oankali to 'awaken' the other survivors of the holocaust whom the Oankali have rescued and kept alive in organic storage pods, and then to prepare them for their return to Earth, now restored by the gene traders. Jdahya, the Oankali who awakened Lilith, tells her that humanity has a 'mismatched pair of genetic characteristics' (39) which effectively prevented it from avoiding self-destruction:

'You are intelligent', he said. 'That's the newer of the two characteristics, and the one you might have put to work to save yourselves. You are potentially one of the most intelligent species we've found, though your focus is different from ours. Still, you had a good start in the life sciences, and even in genetics.'
'What's the second characteristic?'
'You are hierarchical. That's the older and more entrenched characteristic. We saw it in your closest animal relatives and in your most distant ones. It's a terrestial characteristic . . .
And a complex combination of genes that work together to make you intelligent as well as hierarchical will still handicap you whether you acknowledge it or not.'
'I just don't believe it's that simple. Just a bad gene or two.'
'It isn't simple, and it isn't a gene or two. It's many – the result of a tangled combination of factors that only begins with genes.' (39–40)

Some of the other 'factors', which are located in the realms of the cultural and social, are suggested by Lilith's reaction towards the alien Oankali. When Lilith first sees Jdahya, she assumes 'he' is male, and thinks she sees the 'shadowy figure of a man, thin and long-haired' (10). Her response is determined by a patriarchal frame of reference within which masculinity is unambiguously equated with power: even when the 'male' is alien and other, Lilith prefers to think of it as 'he'. However, this patriarchal frame of reference is undermined through a complex piece of textual irony. Once Lilith sees Jdahya clearly, she realises how inappropiate it is to think of him in human terms: she is so appalled by his head and body tentacles that in her terror she reaches back to the patriarchal myth of Medusa to describe him, thus situating him as masculinity's Other. Thus the narrative almost immediately begins to unsettle the hierarchical and patriarchal assumptions about gendered and racial difference which are embedded in the science fiction convention of the alien. Not only does the male alien Jdahya 'parent' Lilith, but she herself then takes on that role for the other humans, male and female, that she has to awaken.

In this novel of shifting boundaries and cultural expectations, the absolute otherness most usually ascribed to women is transferred to the alien. The alien thus becomes the means by which a necessary textual dislocation can be engendered in the narrative which enables the construction of identity, in terms of gender and race, to be explored in the text. Narrative expectations are disrupted by the fact that the alien race is presented as rescuer of the human race rather than its destroyer, as has most often been the case in science fiction. They are further disrupted by the fact that a black woman character occupies the central space of the narrative rather than the peripheries, in contrast to the position that is occupied most often by black women characters, which Sondra O'Neale describes as 'always on the fringes of society, always alone'.[10] If the ambition of the trilogy is to present the possibility of the historic 'reconstruction' of humanity in unwilling partnership with an alien race, then Lilith's role in the narrative is to articulate the difficulties inherent in any new structure of cultural exchange that might result from such a reconstruction. Alternative constructions of difference and identity, race and gender are presented as being central to the terms under which such an exchange would be conducted.

Butler's exploration of these utopian possibilities is complex, however, since she explicitly distances her writing from the presentation of utopian visions of the future, saying that 'personally, I find utopias ridiculous. We're not going to have a perfect human society until we get a few perfect humans, and that seems unlikely.'[11] In common with much contemporary science fiction, Butler's work contains both utopian and dystopian elements, an aspect of the genre which is discussed in more detail in Chapter 4. Despite her assertion to the contrary, Butler's works nevertheless 'strengthen and enrich the feminist utopian tradition in SF', as Hoda Zaki suggests.[12] What the *Xenogenesis* trilogy clearly indicates is that the process of demolishing existing boundaries in order to begin any kind of restructuring is accompanied by equal measures of pleasure and pain.

Lilith is chosen by the Oankali for the 'parenting' role of awakening the other humans because she is 'someone who desperately doesn't want the responsibility, who doesn't want to lead, who is a woman' (164). This depiction of Lilith's particular kind of resistence is especially important in the novel. Although this is the only time that it is referred to in such an explicit way, the narrative suggests that it is her marginality, articulated in terms of both gender and race, that has become her strength. It is Lilith's assertion of her difference, and, ironically enough, of her marginality, that allows her to retain her sense of selfhood by refusing to become fully assimilated within the Oankali, as some of the rescued humans have been. She constantly thinks of resistance and escape, and when 'training' the other humans for their new life on Earth, she urges them to take the knowledge she is giving them and escape from the Oankali once they are returned to Earth.

The ambiguities and difficulties of Lilith's chosen position are used by Butler to attempt to map out the complex cultural relations implied in the oppositions of insider and ousider, centre and margins. Lilith's culturally marginal position as a black woman suggests that Butler is ambivalent about the power relations implicit in the 'intelligent but hierarchical' thesis regarding human behaviour put forward by the Oankali in the narrative. The Oankali choice of Lilith as first 'parent' reinforces this ambivalence, particularly since it ironically overturns another patriarchal myth of origin in which Lilith is Adam's unsatisfactory and disobedient first wife. Butler herself has remarked on the choice of name for her central character, saying 'I like to use names that work with who my characters are.'[13]

In making Lilith central to the narrative development of *Dawn*, Butler emphasises the necessity for an alternative set of power relations based on recognition of difference rather than hierarchy. The relations between Lilith, the other humans and the Oankali focus on the difficulties of establishing such an alternative, and Lilith's role in the narrative draws attention to some of the contradictions.

These contradictions are expressed particularly acutely at the level of sexual relations. Despite her desire for humanity to escape from the Oankali, Lilith does take an Oankali mate, as do other humans. In an attempt to move away from the dominant ideologies of heterosexuality and the family, Butler suggests that 'gene trading' and reproduction can take place only within triads consisting of two human partners and an ooloi, the third Oankali gender. The ooloi are the gene manipulators whose role is to ensure the right 'mix' of genetic ingredients from both humans and Oankali; they also provide their partners with intense physical pleasure and emotional stability. Families consist of five parents, a male and female human, a male and female Oankali and an ooloi. While these extended and non-hierarchical family networks are presented as a potential alternative, Butler does not suggest that they are free from the difficulties common to all other aspects of human–Oankali relations. After all, the Oankali have taken their own measures to ensure that the gene trade will take place: all the rescued humans have been sterilised and it is only through the intercession of an ooloi that conception can occur. Those humans who refuse such contact remain sterile.

Butler presents the human resistence to the Oankali as a contradictory combination of xenophobia and heroism, because the desire for self-determination is ultimately self-defeating. Despite this, Lilith is still regarded as a traitor to humanity by the 'resisters', those humans who have been resettled on Earth but who refuse all contact with the Oankali. Lilith's role in the narrative is to argue through the relative advantages and disadvantages of the exchange. Not only are the Oankali more knowledgeable and therefore more powerful than the remaining humans, but they also have control over reproduction and therefore ultimately over the future of the human race. Although the Oankali establish mixed human–Oankali 'trade partner settlements' (212) many humans reject all that the Oankali offer them on the grounds that the social structures and processes that would be erected actually duplicate a version of slavery. Butler recalls the history and power structures of slavery in the trilogy, as she does in her other books, to situate the discussion of difference and power that is a major focus of the novel.

In the second volume of the trilogy, *Adulthood Rites*, this discussion is explored through the tension between the human–Oankali 'trade settlements' and the resister villages. Although the Oankali leave the resisters alone, there is little comprehension of the human fear that the gene trade will mean the end of humanity, particularly since Oankali survival depends on that trade. Butler's own ambivalence towards the power relations inherent in the human–Oankali exchange emerges in the narrative when the pain felt by the human resisters at their inability to determine their own future is voiced not by Lilith, or any other human, but by Akin, Lilith's human–Oankali child:

> Who among the Oankali was speaking for the interests of resister Humans? Who had seriously considered that it might not be enough to let Humans choose either union with the Oankali or sterile lives free of the Oankali? Trade-village Humans said it, but they were so flawed, so genetically contradictory that they were often not listened to.
>
> He did not have their flaw. He had been assembled within the body of an ooloi. He was Oankali enough to be listened to by other Oankali and Human enough to know that resister Humans were being treated with cruelty and condescension.[14]

In fact, the relations of power shift constantly in the novels: to begin with, Lilith is powerless and alone amongst the Oankali, a position which replicates the cultural position of black women in the dominant culture, but she then becomes a powerful figure in the narrative whose position can no longer be described in terms of those dominant power structures. The alien Oankali are non-hierarchical and represent an alternative set of power structures: although they appear to be in a position of power over the humans, relations of domination are of no interest to them. The way in which Butler represents the Oankali relationship with their human partners is ambiguous: although they appear to exert ultimate control over the eventual fate of the humans, they are at the same time enmeshed in that relationship because of their need to trade genes. There is an ambiguity about the human–Oankali relations of power throughout the trilogy, which Butler attempts to resolve by referring to the Oankali fascination with the 'otherness' of humanity. The Oankali find humanity irresistible from a genetic point of view: Lilith's cancer, which is cured by the Oankali, is regarded as a great gift by them because of the knowledge it provides. Butler uses the metaphor of gene trading to re-examine the culturally specific nature of definitions of otherness and the accompanying relations of power, and these relations and hierarchies of power become increasingly unworkable as the opposition between alien and other breaks down.

Considerable emphasis is placed on the role of reproduction in the narrative because control over reproductive technology is a key issue in any political struggle for autonomy. The inter-related questions of reproduction, regeneration and replication in order to explore the way in which the definition of cultural and sexual others is dependent on the relationship between reproduction, pleasure, and power. The power of regeneration seems to be in the hands of the Oankali, since they can increase human longevity and eliminate disease in the individual. Similarly, power over reproduction is in the control of the Oankali – Lilith is made pregnant by her ooloi partner when it 'knows' she is ready, despite Lilith's own opposition to the idea. This is an uncomfortable echo of the way in which women have had to endure the physical and psychic assault that forcible insemination represents, and is a potentially threatening aspect of human–Oankali relations hardly belied by Butler's depiction of them as non-hierarchical. The power over replication is also in their control since human-Oankali children, or 'constructs' as they are known, are genetically mixed by the ooloi. The Oankali have altered the rules of the game to such an extent that the whole basis of the relationship between pleasure and power has changed. Butler seems to be suggesting that the hierarchies of centre and margins, of coloniser and colonised, of alien and other, no longer provide an appropriate or adequate vocabulary with which to articulate the possibilities for change.

In order that this can be pursued further, the emphasis has to shift from Lilith to her children, who are human–Oankali 'constructs': Akin, who is male, is central to *Adulthood Rites*, and the narrative of *Imago* focuses on Jodahs, who is ooloi. This shift enables Butler to explore the possibilities of those partial and fluid cyborg identities and subject positions proposed by Donna Haraway, in which the 'permanently partial identities and contradictory stand-points' of the cyborg have the potential to enable one to 'see from both perspectives at once because each reveals both dominations and possibilities unimaginable from the other vantage point'.[15] Lilith's children are used in the narrative to suggest that the suppression of difference is a hierarchical strategy by means of which intra-species sex can be represented as an unacceptable dilution of and affront to sameness. The constructs are the result of genetic manipulation and until full maturity or 'metamorphosis' is reached, the children have enough human characteristics to enable those humans who wish to, not to see their Oankali features. Their emergence into full maturity results in a further redefinition of identity, as the constructs choose which gender they wish to become according to whether they are most drawn to male, female or ooloi.

The shift of emphasis in the trilogy from Lilith to the constructs enables Butler to move away from a cultural map that is dependent on familiar oppositions between human and alien, male and female. She uses the constructs to explore a range of subject positions that are outside those oppositions, although her questioning of the heterosexual dominant is confined to the construction of a third gender, which evades the issue somewhat. The stress on hetero-sexuality decreases as attention shifts from Lilith to her construct children. Although non-heterosexual relations in the narrative are mediated through the notion of a third gender, the fixity of subject positions is questioned and hierarchies based on gender and difference become increasingly ambiguous and unsustainable as the question of who is the alien is pursued in the novels. In contrast to the emerging networks of human–Oankali relations, the narrative depicts the human-only partnerships found in resister villages in terms of an unquestioned heterosexuality.

Butler does not altogether seem to endorse the heterosexual dominant, however, since those relations are presented in the narrative as literally non-productive, that is, they are physically sterile because they continue to be structured around expectations that are no longer meaningful. Without the Oankali, humans cannot reproduce. In general, though, Butler does not directly question heterosexual relations, instead they are constantly compared to the sexual relationships of the Oankali. Since the ooloi intercede in all sexual relations, Butler uses the new sexual configuration of human–ooloi relations as a device to raise the possiblity of definitions of desire other than those which are determined by heterosexuality and the family. In *Imago*, the human–ooloi Jodahs mates with a human brother and sister, just as other ooloi mate with their Oankali siblings. Butler is here exploring the possibility outlined by Donna Haraway, that 'some other order of difference might be possible in *Xenogenesis* that could never be born in the Oedipal family'.[16]

Butler explores the possibilities for an alternative 'order of difference' through the constructs rather than through any of the humans, because their human–Oankali identities are hybrids that are outside the determining structures of either culture, and as such they cannot be contained. The greatest contrast in the trilogy is between the hybrid identity of the constructs and that of the humans who have continued to reject the Oankali. The humans have been given longevity but not fertility, and without that focus their lives have become increasingly dispersed, random and unfulfilled. For them, the restored Earth has become an alien space within which they cannot find the key to meaning. Butler's open-ended and ultimately utopian solution to the problem is to allow these humans a final chance to prove that they can break out of the 'intelligent but hierarchical' contradiction by leaving the Earth altogether. The Oankali restore their fertility and, with the guidance of the construct male Akin, they will terra-form Mars, which will become their home planet. In other words, in order to preserve their version of humanity, they have to become the aliens. The reliability of borders is consistently challenged in the trilogy through the metaphors of gene trade, which is about negotiating with borders, and hybrid-isation, which is the creative result of that negotiation. New forms of identity cut across the cultural authority which the ideologies of race and gender claim for themselves. Butler's transformed and hybrid identities begin to dismantle the totalising power structures on which those ideologies rest.

In her other fiction, Butler uses familiar SF metaphors such as time travel, telepathy and mutation to explore the implications for identity and difference of boundary breakdown. Mutation allows for the development of a new kind of selfhood in which difference is not seen to diminish but to fulfil. It implies connection rather than severence by suggesting that sameness and difference are integral parts of a whole rather than binary opposites. Mutation is the dominant metaphor in *Clay's Ark*. The narrative is set in a near-future America in which social and psychic divisions between rich and poor, insiders and outsiders, have more or less solidified into those who live in protected enclaves, and the 'sewer rats' who live in gangland territories or who travel the decaying remains of the state highways. The 'Ark' of the title is the name of an exploratory spacecraft, the crew of which contracted a disease from the planet of Proxima Centauri; when the ship returned to Earth, it blew up, leaving the ship's black geologist as the sole survivor. Eli, since he has also been infected by the disease, is the host for an alien organism and he is driven by the needs of the organism to infect others. Those who survive the severe effects of the initial infection find that the organism has changed their metabolism, enhancing strength and speed and heightening all the senses. It also produces a voracious appetite for food and sexual contact. It even cures disease. Butler emphasises that these are the results of the combination of the alien cells with human cells: 'The organism doesn't use cells up the way a virus does. It combines with them, lives with them, divides with them, changes them just a little. Eli says its a symbiont, not a parasite.' (37) The dissolution of the boundaries between the human and the alien explored in this narrative was later developed by Butler in the *Xenogenesis* trilogy.

The narrative is divided into 'Past' and 'Present', and the 'Past' shows us the progress of the small desert community which contains the first people to be infected by Eli. The only members of the community to survive are three women and for a time Eli enjoys a wholly patriarchal relationship with them: 'Without meaning to, he had enjoyed the harem feeling the three women gave him' (87). Butler ironically undermines the mythic power of the male that is implied here by suggesting that it is the reproductive drive of the organism that is controlling Eli's sexual needs rather than his own patriarchal urge to power:

> He would not give the organism another fragment of himself, of his humanity. He would not let it make him a stud with three mares. He would make a colony, an enclave on the ranch. A human gathering, not a herd. (87)

This establishes yet another version of the complex cycle of regeneration and reproduction that appears throughout Butler's fiction, where the narratives struggle to articulate some form of community that is not based on a version of the nuclear family and that can accommodate difference.

In those sections of the narrative that are described as the 'Present', Butler uses the transitional nature of the community and its inhabitants to depict the gradual transformation of humanity into something other than human. The community isolates itself in an attempt to contain the spread of the organism, abducting the occasional traveller when driven by the needs of the organism for contact with more 'hosts'. There is a constant struggle to keep a balance between the demands of the organism and the community's sense of being human. As one of the members of the community explains to a newly contaminated member of the group: 'We're changed, but we have ethics. We aren't animals' (37). The tension between sameness and difference, and the different kinds of relations that this might imply for new forms of community, suggests that Butler does not underestimate the enormous difficulties that might be involved in coming to terms with such differences. This is made clear in the narrative when one of the infected males takes his own life rather than accept the changes resulting from the organism:

> He talked about the impossibility of spending his life as the carrier of a deadly disease. He talked about his fear of losing himself, becoming someone or something else. He talked about courage and cowardice and confusion. Finally, he put the letters aside and cheated the microbe of the final few days it needed to tighten its hold on him. He took one of Meda's sharp butcher knives and cut his throat. (134)

The tension between sameness and difference is emphasised by the fact that the children born into this community are not human in the same way, they are a new species, another form of hybrid identity. The human characteristics of the parents have, therefore, a kind of built-in obsolescence, as is the case in much of Butler's fiction. Although preservation of sameness is abandoned in the interests of a kind of on-going development and change, Butler conveys this somewhat unexpectedly in terms of biological determinism rather than the shifting power relations of race and gender:

> 'We're the future', he said simply. 'We're the sporangia of the dominant life form of Proxi Two – the receptacles that produce the spores of that life form. If we survive, *if our children survive*, it will be because we fulfill our purpose – because we spread the organism.' (181)

The disturbing implications of the biological image become clear in the narrative, as the organism's drive to reproduce itself means that the inevitable outcome for women is not a shift in gendered power relations but permanent pregnancy, whether it is desired or not:

> 'When we've changed', he said, 'when the organism "decides"

whether or not we're going to live, it shares the differences it's found
in us with others who have changed. . . . We had a woman who had
had herself sterilized before we got her – had her tubes cauterized.
Her organisms communicated with Meda's and her tubes opened up.
She's pregnant now.' (195)

Although it is presented in terms of the 'chemical exchanges' that
are negotiated by the organism, sexuality and female desire clearly
remain unresolved issues in *Clay's Ark*, a feature common to other
narratives by Butler.

From their relative safety in the desert, the community begins
to hear reports of the burning of towns and cities in America and
the rest of the world. Despite the ambiguity of the biological
metaphor used by Butler to describe the process by which humanity
becomes other to itself, she does make some attempt to counteract
it at the end of the narrative by reworking the opposition between
human/uninfected and alien/infected, in terms of the threat represented by difference:

> Fires are being set everywhere. Maybe uninfected people are
> sterilizing the city in the only way they can think of. Or maybe it's
> infected people crazy with their symptoms. . . . In Louisiana there's a
> group that has decided the disease was brought in by foreigners – so
> they're shooting anyone who seems a little odd to them. Mostly
> Asians, blacks, and browns. (200)

As in all of Butler's work, the narrative is open-ended, and closure
around the familiar distinctions between sameness and difference,
power and powerlessness, becomes impossible.

The Patternist novels have a similar focus on the emergence of
a new and therefore incomplete identity based on unresolved
tensions between race and gender. In *Mind of my Mind* and *Wild
Seed* the 'alien' presence through which the limits of identity are
explored is more ambiguous and more centrally related to what
Stuart Hall has referred to as the 'diasporia experience and its
narratives of displacement'.[17] The power relations of race and
gender are examined through the metaphors of telepathy and mind
transfer, which, like the alien, represent both a threat to sameness
and the possibility of imagining other forms of social and sexual
relations. The narrative of *Mind of my Mind* centres on the power
struggle between Mary, a young Afro-American woman who has
powerful telepathic abilities, and Doro, her genetic father. Doro is

a four thousand year old Nubian, a genetic mutant who has the power to transfer his psychic essence from one host to another. He has been selectively breeding his children for generations in order to build a new and superior race. He thinks of Mary as the culmination of this long breeding programme, and after her 'transition' from a latent to an active telepath, he is ready to use her to ensure the final coming into being of his empire, with himself as patriarchal head. The narrative is an exploration of the differences between their attitudes towards power. Both are in a sense parasites, feeding off others for their power. Doro is compelled to 'take' people's minds in order to inhabit their bodies. He controls 'his' people through fear and does what he wants with them, since he considers that they belong to him.

Butler is concerned with the sexual as well as the psychic relations of power and, as in the *Xenogenesis* novels, the narrative confronts the incest taboo as part of the questioning of the universal validity of Oedipal conflict. Doro makes love to Mary and then marries her off to Karl, one of his telepathically active white sons, so they can begin to 'breed'. It is Karl who wonders,

> Had human life ever mattered to Doro beyond his interest in human husbandry? Could a creature who had to look upon ordinary people literally as food and shelter ever understand how strongly those people valued life? But yes, of course he could. He understood it well enough to use it to keep his people in line. . . . It just didn't make any difference. He didn't care.[18]

Incest taboos are dealt with somewhat ambiguously because Doro is able to use different bodies in his sexual relations with his children, but the fact that these relations are based on power is made clear. Mary herself says of sex with Doro, 'I probably loved him in self-defense. Hating him was too dangerous' (34).

Mary's telepathic power is such that she can draw people into her mental 'pattern' and once there they cannot get free. They become part of her 'mind'. But the mental link is liberating as well as confining, since she uses it to help other latent telepaths to become active and adds them to the pattern. Although the relations between Mary and the other telepaths are unequal, much as they are between the Oankali and the humans in the *Xenogenesis* trilogy, Butler always presents the sets of new and developing relations as a preferable option to what existed before. In *Xenogenesis*, humans had no future without the Oankali; in *Mind of my Mind*, the latent telepaths in Mary's mental web were invariably victims or perpetrators of child abuse, and other forms of mental and physical abuse, and Mary 'heals' these social and psychic victims in the process of claiming them for her pattern. In all these narratives, within which the law of the father is resisted, the stress is on the transformative quality of the new relations. Thus, Mary's 'pattern' replaces Doro's patriarchal empire with something that establishes a living network of mutual interdependence, in contrast to the repressive patriarchal structures imposed by Doro. The daughter becomes a rival to the father but instead of submitting to him, Mary engages in psychic battle with Doro and kills him, not as some kind of heroic individual but by drawing on the power of this network.

Mary's telepathic community represents a collective human experience in which both colonial and Oedipal narratives are gone beyond; relations of power are rethought so that the emphasis falls on the struggle to achieve what Fred Pfeil calls 'an unprecedented unity-with-difference',[19] in which cultural identity is open to transformation. However, Butler finally leaves the question of unequal power relations unresolved in the narrative, since they include not only those between Mary and the others in the web, but also those which exist between the telepaths and the ordinary humans who are referred to dismissively as 'mutes'. Since their main role is imagined as being to help those with special latent abilities through their difficult 'transition' periods, the narrative is in danger of repeating the very structures of control and repression that it sought to replace. This is partly due to Butler's expressed lack of interest in presenting utopian solutions, but ironically enough it is also due to the fact that neither Mary nor Doro are sufficiently alien to allow Butler to explore fully the question of difference. The lack of resolution and closure does mean, however, that Mary's narrative position remains pivotal, which ensures that both race and gender remain central to any rethinking of the relations of power, however tentative that may be.

In *Wild Seed*, the slave narrative that is implicit in Doro's breeding empire is further explored. Although it was published after *Mind of my Mind*, the narrative fills out much of the detail of how Doro organises the genetic breeding programme which is described there, by situating it in that period of history when the African slave trade was at its height. In an imitation of that trade Doro has 'seed villages' in Africa where he breeds his children and then ships the most promising off to the colony he has established in the New World to join his breeding programme. Although they do not live as slaves there, neither are they free, and the narrative draws a parallel between Doro's patriarchal attitude towards his people and that of white slave owners towards their slaves. The 'wild seed' of the title is Anyanwu; she is a powerful healer and shape changer who has already lived for three hundred years without being discovered, and therefore controlled, by Doro. When he does find her he immediately wants her incorporated into his breeding programme, and persuades her to accompany him to America with the promise that together they will have children who will no longer die before she does. In fact, he wants to breed her in exactly the same way that he breeds all his other people, and it is her struggle to resist his power that becomes the subject of the narrative.

As in *Mind of my Mind*, the narrative explores the discourses of power but also the way in which they can be resisted, and in a sense it is the feminisation of power that is the real issue in the novels. Doro's masculinised version of power is manifested in his desire to possess and to control through fear. Although Anyanwu is the only person he has ever discovered who has the same longevity as himself, he cannot accept that her power makes her an equal. Her difference is a threat and as such she is to be used and discarded:

> He would have to teach her, instruct her quickly and begin using her at once. He wanted as many children as he could get from her before it became necessary to kill her. Wild seed always had to be destroyed eventually. It could never conform as children born among his people conformed. (80)

It is Doro's use of power that confirms his lack of humanity, not his other strangeness. His insistence on conformity from all those strange others in his control is an irony pursued by Butler in the narrative.

Anyanwu's feminisation of power consists of a process not of expansion but of containment, both of herself and Doro. Doro forces her into marriage with his son Isaac, and although Isaac pursuades her to submit to Doro, the relations of power are explicitly described in terms of slavery:

> She knew now how the slaves had felt as they lay chained on the bench, the slaver's hot iron burning into their flesh. In her pride, she

had denied that she was a slave. She could no longer deny it. Doro's
mark had been on her from the day they met. She could break free of
him only by dying and sacrificing her children and leaving him loose
upon the world to become even more of an animal. (116)

She submits to him, bears children at his direction, and protects those
around her from his malign influence as well as she can. She refuses
the option of confrontation, since it would result in her own death
or that of her children, neither of which would change the structure
of the power relations in which she and others more vulnerable than
her are enmeshed. However, she resists characterisation as a victim
of oppression through her ability to shape-change, which allows her
to cross and recross the borders between nature and culture, race
and gender, at will.

Anyanwu escapes from Doro's uncanny ability to track her by
shape-changing into animal form, and disappearing into the 'chinks'
of the world. Doro does not find her for another hundred years, by
which time she has established her own community of those who are
'misfits, malcontents, troublemakers'. Where Doro's communities
are based on the patriarchal power relations of domination and
repression, hers is a gathering of 'slightly strange ones' who treat her
as 'mother, older sister, teacher and, when she invited it, lover' (196).
This community and her relationship to those in it is a demonstration
of the feminisation of power, as is the fact that her people seem to
produce as many special abilities as any of Doro's breeding
programmes have done.

When Doro begins to exert his control over her community and
'kills' one of the members of it for his own satisfaction, Anyanwu's
response is one that makes sense in the context of the feminisation
of power. In the face of Doro's refusal to make any accommodation
with her, she decides to manipulate her body in order to die, rather
than watch him turn her community into one based on coercion and
fear. Only the prospect of such irrevocable loss forces Doro to
recognise the need for change and compromise:

> He did not command her any longer. She was no longer one of his
> breeders, nor even one of his people in the old proprietary way. He
> could ask her cooperation, her help, but he could no longer coerce her
> into giving it. There would be no more threats to her children. (247)

An important aspect of Butler's fiction is its refusal to offer 'magical'
resolutions of difficulties and contradictions, and the narrative

therefore avoids any sense of closure around their transformed relationship. The uneasy compromise between Anyanwu and Doro is a crucial pointer to those possibilities for on-going change and development with which all of Butler's fiction is concerned: 'There had to be changes. Anyanwu could not have all she wanted, and Doro could no longer have all that he had once considered his by right' (247). Butler's sparse prose underlines the intensity of the struggle to overcome patriarchal notions of ownership and control, manifested through the master/slave relations which permeate the social and sexual relations in the novel.

The Patternist novels, like the *Xenogenesis* trilogy, are concerned with the dissolving of the boundaries of the body and with the remaking of identity. The dualities between male and female, black and white, human and animal, that form the framework for repression and domination become more fluid. While away from Doro, Anyanwu changes her shape to become a young white male; while she is a man she marries a white woman who then bears their children. When Doro finds her, she is a woman, and so he comes to her in the body of a black male that he knows will please her. The distinction that is made in *Wild Seed* between the different ways in which Doro and Anyanwu maintain their longevity raises the issue of the gendering of power. Doro's existence depends on the 'taking' of bodies, so, for him, possession and power are inseparable; Anyanwu is able to regenerate and recreate her own body, thus avoiding the relations of oppression that are crucial to Doro's existence. The tension between these opposing versions of power is present in various stages of irresolution in both Patternist books. Much of the pleasure of reading them comes from the way in which this irresolution creates a space for the elaboration of those conditions of existence necessary for the 'cyborg monsters' of feminist science fiction proposed by Donna Haraway, which 'define quite different political possibilities and limits from those proposed by the mundane fiction of Man and Woman'.[20]

The Postmodern Aliens of Gwyneth Jones

The contradictory fear of and desire for the other is central to Gwyneth Jones' elegant and ironic 'first contact' narrative, *White Queen* (1991). Where Octavia Butler's work is often marked by what Adele Newson has called a 'characteristic ambivalence toward her message',[21] Jones is fully aware of and exploits the ambiguity that resides in conflicting definitions of identity, and in so doing undermines the binary construction of those definitions. The science fiction convention of the alien attempts to present otherness in unitary terms, so that 'humanity' is uncomplicatedly opposed to the 'alien'; both Jones and Butler focus on the way in which that opposition seeks to supress the others of both gender and race by subsuming them within a common-sense notion of what it is to be human. Like Butler, Jones is interested in the transformative potential of the interactions between self and other, as well as the difficulties inherent in such transformations.

At this point, the similarities between the two writers end, since Jones has a fundamentally different perspective on the genre: she uses the familiar science fiction device of the alien against the genre itself, by parodying the entire process of first contact as well as the essentialist distinction between sameness and difference with which the device and the genre are infused. Instead of stressing the differences between humans and aliens, Jones ironically reverses the emphasis and stresses the similarities. She inverts the conventions of the genre in order to diminish the distance between human and alien, so that the particular ways in which science fiction narratives have operated to suppress otherness can be explored. *White Queen* is a contradictory narrative in the sense in which Linda Hutcheon uses the term to describe postmodernism, in that it is a text that 'uses and abuses, installs and then subverts, the very concepts it challenges'.[22]

The information-saturated near-future environment created by Jones is described in terms that are deliberately reminiscent of the most apocryphal fears of the contemporary present: 'The '04 was supposed to be the great environmental catastrophe, God's punishment for the human race's misdeeds' (63). There is a weary familiarity to this future which draws attention to the way in which science fiction narratives are always, in a particular sense, about the present:

> Cold and famine took the world that had been preparing for hot flushes and rising seas. . . . Everyone got ready to die. But in a few years it was as if nothing had happened. The human race, somewhat rearranged, carried on getting and spending, making politics, having fun. Starving and suffering if anything a little less, just now. . . . (48)

Although the constituent parts of this near future are clearly recognisable, Jones has introduced some ironic additions and differences; microchip technology has been replaced by a 'living' substance called 'coralin', on which the world's information networks are now based. Old viruses, such as AIDS, remain, but there are also some new ones, such as QV, a computer virus which has become a literal rather than a virtual infection; since the virus can be transferred from human carrier to coralin, those who are carriers of the virus are excluded from any access to the information networks. China and Japan have united, and a socialist revolution has just taken place in the United States, which declares itself to be the United Socialist States of America, although the news has less impact than might have been expected: 'It would have been the story of the century, wonderful movie-drama, if the aliens had not arrived' (131). This same-but-different characteristic of the narrative gives Jones the opportunity to situate the human–alien encounter within familiar expectations and assumptions which can then be re-examined, as can the way in which they are reproduced within science fiction narratives.

As the humans and aliens struggle to establish some form of meaningful communication, all the viewpoints in the narrative are presented as both limited and provisional, with the result that no narrative voice or perspective emerges as dominant. It is a significant feature of the narrative that the struggle for meaning is shown to take place within both the human and the alien groupings, as well as across them. There is a constant sense of movement in the narrative, not only between geographical locations but, more significantly, between the human and the alien interpretation of events, and because those interpretations never seem to coincide fully, meanings can be shown to be negotiable and subject to dispute. Definitions of difference constantly shift from the alien to the human: somewhat disconcertingly, the aliens speak in fully idiomatic English, and while the humans refer to the visitors as 'the aliens', the aliens ironically refer to the humans as 'the locals'.

Jones directs considerable irony towards the essentialism of science fiction narratives through which meanings are assumed to be both fixed and universal, by focusing on the mismatch between human and alien understanding of the social and cultural meanings inscribed in language:

But they spoke in proverbs, sometimes they made no sense whatever. The term 'Aleutian' was a case in point. It remained current, because

> when asked the real name of their planet, or their native country they
> replied with enthusiasm, 'Aleutia!' The names by which they were
> known were of the same uncertain provenance. They had emerged
> from a succession of alternatives: Rajath had been 'Duke' at one time;
> also 'Hanuman'; Lugha had been 'Coyote'. The SETI database had
> called them 'Sanskrit-like terms', which was exciting for those who
> believed that the human race was a lost tribe of some great galactic
> race. (98–9)

Because the Aleutian distinction between formal and informal
speech is not recognised, what is intended by the Aleutian use of
proverbs cannot be understood, and the non-verbal informal speech
is thought to be telepathy.

This gap in comprehension is rendered in appropriately
postmodernist terms in the narrative as Clavel, one of the Aleutians,
explains that 'You people see our signifiers, users of formal language,
as rulers. . . . We don't have rulers. We are, I think, an *anarchy*'
(307). The narrative is structured around ironic reversals which
function at the expense of dominant cultural attitudes, in particular
towards information technology. The aliens have an appropriately
'alien' view of information technology, and although they are
completely familiar with the systems, they also revere them and
invest them with mystical properties, believing those humans who
are most involved with the technology to be 'priests' who live
'surrounded by ghosts, ruled utterly by commands and portents
from the spirit world' (83). Baudrillard's assertion that the real is
being replaced by the simulated is here given ironic and somewhat
unsympathetic expression as a form of transcendental mysticism.

In the encounters between humans and aliens, Jones exposes the
way in which science fiction notions of the alien are fed by and feed
into a range of cultural and social myths of the alien and the other,
with the result that an utterly contradictory set of assumptions about
origins is promulgated. The way in which these assumptions inform
all aspects of the contemporary post-colonial and post-industrial
environment is explored in the narrative, and at the same time the
way in which science fiction narratives themselves reproduce those
assumptions is revealed. The science fiction metaphor of the alien is
constantly used against itself in the narrative in order to undermine
assumptions about race and gender in particular. The humans who
meet the aliens are shown to be so enmeshed in those assumptions
that every version of the human–alien contact is skewed by the

framework within which it is perceived; the same is true for the alien version of that encounter. By presenting both the human and the alien accounts of the same incidents, Jones can emphasise the way in which narratives of difference are necessarily constructed from the materials to hand, in other words, from whatever cultural and political imperatives are dominant.

The dominance of a hierarchical myth of origins means that humans immediately believe the aliens to be a race of telepathic superbeings:

> It could be taken for granted that they had faster than light drive of some kind. Wormholes, some way of tying knots in the galactic spaghetti. This was no suprise. It was a truism that the aliens who landed, whoever they were, *had to be superior*. Or else we'd be visiting them. (69)

This view ironically rehearses assumptions that are built into many science fiction narratives about the inevitably hierarchical relations that must ensue in human–alien encounters, as well revealing the way in which science fiction itself is implicated in the reproduction of such hierarchies. As the narrative presents the alien perspective on the encounter, the references to FTL travel and associated science fictional images become increasingly ironic and iconoclastic; in defiance of science fiction conventions, these aliens have not journeyed from their home planet using FTL technology, because they do not have FTL technology. The ship in which they have travelled is simply parked out of sight behind the moon, waiting for them to return from what was supposed to have been a profitable trading mission that has proved more lucrative than expected, because of the utter susceptibility of human culture to its own myths. While humans attempt to give transcendental qualities to the aliens, the aliens are working out how to extract more profit from the situation: 'Let me try this on you. Today, when the priests come, one of them insults us. We require compensation. We take it in the form of property rights. We sell at an immense profit and take home the loot' (91). The profit motive itself is not unfamiliar, except when expressed by aliens who have the look of angels, with their 'idealised, ungendered bodies from a stained glass window' (143).

When the mutual incomprehension escalates so that war seems imminent, the similarities and differences between humans and aliens become apparent: the humans assume that the visiting

Aleutians represent their whole 'nation', whereas the real position is that they are 'private adventurers. . . . This expedition doesn't have big backers. It is marginal' (139). The eventual peace-making overtures of the Aleutians are accordingly misinterpreted by the humans in a way that continues to sustain their own belief system: 'The Aleutians had sued for peace when they had no need to do so, when they had the earth in their power' (144). Not surprisingly, the Aleutian version of the situation is different: 'It's like this. We have nothing from which to build actual weapons' (140). The narrative does not suggest that the other is unknowable, but it does indicate that assumptions or impositions of sameness represent refusals to recognise difference, and that within such refusals lies the terror of the other.

The fear of the dissolution of the self by and in the other is explored through the multilayered relations that develop between Braemar Wilson and Johnny Guglioni, and between both of them and the aliens, in particular Clavel. Although she looks merely middle-aged, Braemar is a sixty-three year old Afrasian grandmother, an 'obsolete housewife' turned television presenter and tabloid journalist; she also has a controlled cancer and is HIV positive. Johnny is an idealistic young American, a former engineer–journalist who believes he has contracted the QV virus. Their identities, needs and desires are explicit reminders of the ambiguous overlap between the contemporary, and the future present of the narrative. Both Johnny and Braemar are in West Africa because of the aliens: Johnny has had a brief, uncomprehending contact with Clavel, and Braemar wants to exploit that contact to get the story on the aliens. Johnny simply hopes that the aliens have some miraculous cure for QV, in the best tradition of science fiction narratives about 'superior' aliens.

In order to gain access to his alien contact, Braemar initiates an intensely erotic but fundamentally exploitative affair with Johnny which develops into a more complex and contradictory relationship: 'The corruption at the heart of their love, the violence and treachery, was as vital as the love itself' (251). Their mutually dependent relationship increasingly acts as a parallel to the way in which relations develop between humans and aliens, and it is through this network of relations that the tension between sameness and difference emerges. This is further emphasised by Clavel's love for Johnny, which is based on a set of premises that involves a different definition of desire, as Braemar explains to Johnny:

Clavel's in love with you, Johnny. Remember how she called you 'Daddy', back in Africa? They believe in reincarnation. A 'Clavel' might be born in every generation. It's their big romantic quest, to find another edition of yourself: 'your 'true' parent or your 'true' child. (201)

Conflicting definitions of desire and difference in the narrative act to prevent closure around the repressive dominance of homogeneity.

Jones undermines the essentialism of the binary divsion between human and alien, self and other, by presenting a view of difference that incorporates contradictions rather than attempting to resolve them, a narrative strategy unfamiliar in science fiction: 'Humans and aliens were so alike. They were two almost identical surfaces, at first glance seamlessly meeting: at a closer look hopelessly just out of sync, in every tiny cog of detail' (309). The narrative explores the difficulties of living with difference through the metaphor of 'White Queen', the name given to itself by a small and elitist terrorist group opposed to the alien presence. In what emerges as an ironic narrative gesture, Braemar, the 'smart Asian matron' (249), has joined White Queen because she fears that the presence of the aliens would mean the inevitable end of 'Everything we ever did, everything we ever made: dead and worse than dead, *meaningless*' (287). Although 'White Queen' appears only towards the end of the novel, it symbolises that repressive terror of the Other which the rest of the narrative has been concerned to deconstruct. It is this fear of the dissolution of the self which provides the rationale for the existence of 'White Queen', and its presence in the narrative is a reminder of the way in which the science fiction narratives of the 1950s were expressive of a particular set of political anxieties. In an allusion to that historical moment, Jones places White Queen in the context of a decaying London that, despite its tropical climate and monsoon flooding, has both the look and feel of the contemporary:

The mood of Braemar's London had been set by the '04. There was no order in the cosmos any more, only the shocking certainty that *anything can happen.* . . . People were waiting for the next global disaster, because catastrophes were normal now . . . anything would do. The neighbour star that goes nova and floods earth with killer radiation, the giant asteroid on a collision course, the new and unstoppable mutated virus, the Night of the Living Dead. . . . This was the world that had abandoned movie-drama and stayed away in droves from the holo-films. Animation, cartoon emotion was the favoured artistic expression. Dramatic realism was too slow, too ordered: completely unlike nature. (168)

In this postmodern context, the aliens become the longed-for crisis, provoking both desire and loathing.

To the wealthy and elite members of White Queen, the aliens are the epitome of otherness, but Braemar's identification with White Queen is more ambiguous. It is placed in the context of a colonialism that was unequivocal about its repression of differences of race and gender:

> She was a little girl again in that great land of heat and birth, sweating in a scratchy uniform from far away. She stood and sang the war songs of a cold, small island, poured her heart out. Wrong skin, wrong sex, wrong culture: but the need to belong was stronger than self-respect. She had always wanted to have adventures, to be brave, to be the hero of her own life. She felt a weight on her shoulders, the armour and the crown. The champion entered the lists, a woman with the heart and stomach of a man.
> And a white man, at that. What shameful nonsense. (289–90)

Braemar's involvement in White Queen is replete with contradictions, as is her relationship with Johnny; the 'weird and oblique morality' (205) that she constructs means that her sense of self depends on an absolute opposition to the visible other, which, in crucial ways, she herself represents. Braemar finally attempts to sabotage the Aleutian mother ship as a last means of resisting the 'invader', and when the attempt fails, she 'condemned herself to live' (303) by letting Johnny be executed by the Aleutians, in order that she can continue her resistance. As he realises this, Johnny is able to articulate, in terms of race and gender, the oppositional relations between heterogeneity and difference, and homogeneity and sameness, that are left unresolved in the narrative: 'He could taste the poison, fear and the abuse of power: between human and alien, between men and women' (299).

The competing narratives in *White Queen*, through which those relations are expressed, are also left unresolved: human–alien relations, characterised as the 'unconsummated wedding, the irremediable almost-matching of two worlds' (310), remain largely as they were, with the aliens partially assimilated within a culture that is unfamiliar and only half understood. Braemar remains unreconciled to the alien presence, only understanding that 'to love one's enemy: to heal the divided self, is not simple' (303), and White Queen continues its guerilla activities, as the ironically re-named 'Oroonoko'. The impossibility of closure in the narrative means that it is both unstable and self-referential, and this enables Jones to suggest possibilities for the development of an alternative framework for thinking about difference, one that is not characterised by polarities and hierarchies, but which is contingent, on the edges of the possible: 'No language matches another, no language models the world. But almost, almost . . . and between the dropped and the caught stitches of that immaterial, impossible weaving somehow: the meaning comes' (310).

Chapter 3

Destabilising Gender and Genre

Vonda McIntyre and C.J. Cherryh both work within the conventional narrative structures of science fiction, and the contradiction between those structures and the feminist intentions of the narratives is addressed in this chapter. Although both writers create strong female characters capable of challenging the assumption that heroism is a defining characteristic of masculinity, the generic conventions within which female heroes are depicted tend to retain their patriarchal inflection. As Anne Cranny-Francis has pointed out, the conventional narrative structure of science fiction is 'extremely problematic for feminist science fiction writers since it encodes a patriarchal discourse which contradicts the feminist discourse operating in the text'.[1] When generic narrative conventions are reworked from an oppositional point of view, assumptions about gender are openly confronted within the narratives, but this does not necessarily lead to an interrogation of the way in which gender itself is constructed. On the other hand, rewriting the conventions from the unexpected and 'alien' perspective of the female subject can work towards providing a critical position from which such an interrogation could begin.

It is not necessary, therefore, to think of the contradictions that are generated in the narratives in entirely negative terms, since the ambivalence and ambiguities of meaning in patriarchal structures can become more obvious when they come into conflict with feminist rewritings. Feminist appropriations are inevitably partial because they remain embedded within the conventional narrative structures

54

of the genre, but they can nevertheless alter the focus of the narratives to reveal the equally embedded nature of the power relations within which the subject is constructed, and which define the relations between self and other. Although 'appropriation' has become a somewhat overworked notion in these postmodern times, it has nevertheless restored a measure of control and 'discrimination', as Meaghan Morris has pointed out: 'In appropriation, the elements chosen, and the choice of elements, are not released in free play or a random heterogeneous "shuffling" in Jameson's phrase, but, on the contrary, weighted with critical, historical, particularizing significance'.[2] Femininist appropriations of science fiction are not, then, incapacitated by the encoding of patriarchal discourse in the generic narrative structures of science fiction: they are cultural interventions which result in texts that are recognisably structured by partiality and difference, rather than unity. Awareness of the power structures inherent in gender relations makes it possible for the writers of feminist science fiction to re-use the conventions of the genre, but not to expel entirely the assumptions about gender and social relations on which those conventions rest. As Jane Flax has indicated,

> Gender relations enter into and are constituent elements in every aspect of human experience. In turn, the experience of gender relations for any person and the structure of gender as a social category are shaped by the interactions of gender relations and other social relations such as class and race.[3]

What the narratives of feminist science fiction can do is to test the limits of the dominant ideology of gender by proposing alternative possibilities for social and sexual relations which conflict with the dominant representations. However, even though the narratives may present strong female heroes or women-only worlds, they can offer only incomplete solutions to the problems of unequal power relations; the narratives themselves are often highly contradictory and marked by what Jameson has called 'generic discontinuities'.

The ambivalence and ambiguity of these narratives introduces elements of instability and uncertainty, a reminder that the reconstruction of gender can take place only in de Lauretis's 'elsewhere', where such partial perspectives are a means of resisting the totalising tendencies of hegemonic discourse.

Vonda McIntyre and the Spatial Experience of Postmodern Otherness

Vonda McIntyre uses the narrative structures and conventions that provide a lot of the pleasure for readers of science fiction to shift the focus of that pleasure away from the conventional expectations about social and sexual relations that are built into such narratives. McIntyre's narratives do not focus on whole societies but only on fragmented parts, and this enables her to suggest an alternative narrative space within which representations of gender can take place. There is no attempt made in the stories to reassemble the parts into a comforting totality within which tensions between social and gender relations are magically eliminated. The distinguishing feature of these narratives is that they remain fragmented and incapable of closure, in contrast to the resolution and closure that is familiar in other SF narratives.

In a discussion of McIntyre's early novel, *The Exile Waiting* (1975; 1985), Fredric Jameson suggests that, in contrast to the linear causality of more 'realistic' narratives, our interest in this novel lies in the way it presents 'spatial experience itself'. In distinguishing between different kinds of SF, he suggests that.

> Space also plays a significant part in the emergence of the newer SF narratives as well. If, as I believe, all SF of the more 'classical' type is 'about' containment, closure, the dialectic of inside and outside, then the generic distinction between those texts and others that have come to be called 'fantasy' (e.g., McIntyre's own *Dreamsnake* [1978]) will also be a spatial one, in which these last are seen as open-air meadow texts of various kinds.[4]

The terms of this discussion relate to Jameson's view that, in the 'new space' of postmodernism, we are confronted with 'the notion of spatialization replacing that of temporalization', which results in 'the loss of our ability to *position ourselves within this space and cognitively map it*'.[5] The notion of 'spatialization' operates as a metaphor for the erosion both of historical consciousness and of the belief that there are deep structures of meaning that underlie appearances. Jameson suggests that this is why science fiction can sometimes offer 'a way of breaking through to history in a new way, achieving a distinctive historical consciousness by way of the future rather than the past, becoming conscious of our present as the past of some unexpected future'.[6]

For Jameson, then, the presentation of 'spatial experience itself' in McIntyre's novel is not only an indication of the historical dislocation that he sees in postmodernism but it is also a means by which the present can be obliquely apprehended. Although Jameson does not acknowledge the question of gender, the way in which spatial experience is presented in McIntyre's narrative significantly challenges the 'containment and closure' of traditional SF texts around fixed definitions of gender. The binarisms around which definitions of the subject and of gender relations are structured become unstable within the 'spatial experience' of postmodernism. This 'spatial experience' is conveyed within McIntyre's narrative through irresolution and the refusal of closure, and thus the narrative can offer a privileged account of the dislocations of postmodernism, but also, and more significantly, it can offer a gendered reading of those dislocations.

A recurring spatial environment in several of McIntyre's novels is that of the 'Centre', a self-enclosed technological environment that has cut itself off almost entirely from the rest of the post-holocaust Earth. In *The Exile Waiting*, the narrative takes place almost entirely in the huge underground city that is the Centre: in *Dreamsnake* (1978; 1979), the narrative is set amongst the various fragmented communities outside the Centre. The image of a 'centre' also occurs in the later novel, *Superluminal* (1983; 1984), although it is referred to there as the 'Administration', an ill-defined but powerful source of authority.[7] These recurring references mark out a set of concerns in the novels that are to do with testing the limits of the boundaries between centre and margins, insider and outsider, self and other.

Few narrative memories of the Centre are provided in any of the novels mentioned, although it is indicated that it is rigidly hierarchical and based on quasi-feudal, in-bred family structures. It exists as an enclosed remnant of earlier patriarchal structures, but without any of the power and authority of those structures. The social and political institutions implied by the idea of a 'Centre' remain curiously disembodied, and in similar fashion the 'Administration' is present only as a kind of totalising bureaucracy which subsumes whole sets of social and sexual relationships within its own unknown and undescribed structures. In each of the novels, the 'centre' is associated with social stagnation, moral decline, and with the suppression of difference in the interests of sameness. Change takes place either outside their static environment or in the sealed-off spaces within them, and because of this, the Centre becomes increasingly irrelevant.

In the post-catastrophe world of *The Exile Waiting* and *Dreamsnake* in particular, new forms of social and sexual relations take place only outside the literal and metaphoric confines of the Centre. Change, development and the acknowledgement of difference are therefore depicted as always taking place away from the centres, at the margins. But since the narratives indicate that the 'Centre' is itself marginal, then 'normal' spatial boundaries are disrupted and become unstable. The textual ambiguities which result are a product of the spatial element in McIntyre's narrative described by Jameson, which prevents closure around the binarisms and hierarchical relations of gender.

In *The Exile Waiting*, the idea of marginality and dispersal features strongly in the narrative. If spatial boundaries are unstable and are disrupted, so, too, are the boundaries of self and other. The three main characters in the story embody this instability as they each struggle with different kinds of psychic fragmentation within the enclosed environment of the Centre, and the Centre itself becomes emblematic of that fragmentation as its increasingly malign influence on the characters is described in the narrative. The central character, Mischa, has telepathic abilities which place her outside the boundaries of the acceptable in the Centre; her abilities are considered a mutation, a difference which is capable of disrupting the binary relation between nature and culture. Although the Centre is itself underground, all mutants are exiled to the even deeper underground tunnels of the city, and the only reason that Mischa has escaped such a fate is that her particular difference is not visible. Mischa is linked to her telepathic but mentally disabled sister, Gemmi, from whose agonisingly incoherent telepathic demands Mischa cannot escape, unless she can go off-planet, and the narrative traces her attempts to get away both from Gemmi and from the stultifying power structures of the Centre. Within those hierarchical relations of power, Mischa is defined as an outsider, and the narrative focuses on her refusal to accept the limitations imposed on her by that definition of difference.

The other major characters are also 'outsiders', in that they come from outside the Centre, and are equally defined by their difference. Subtwo is one of a pair of genetically engineered 'pseudosibs' who have an 'artificial biomechanical link between them'[8] and, with his sib, Subone, he lands on Earth with a party of space raiders which intends to take over the Centre. More importantly, Subtwo is struggling to complete the emotional and psychic separation from his pseudosib that should have taken place long ago. As a genetically engineered human, Subtwo already exists outside the frame of reference provided by the opposition between nature and culture, and this is emphasised by the way in which the biomechanical link between the pseudo-sibs has repressed any real emotional or psychic growth in either of them. The sameness that is imposed by that link parallels the sameness that is imposed by the hierarchical relations of power in the Centre, and it is only by refusing sameness in the interests of difference that Subtwo can begin to develop a sense of self.

Jan arrived with the raiding party, although he is not part of their plan to take over the Centre. He had been accompanying his much-loved companion, an old, blind space navigator, because she wanted to return to Earth to die. Jan is also an alienated outsider who has been unable to establish a sense of connection with anyone except the now dead navigator. The narrative suggests that it is Jan's difference that has alienated him from his father, and that the rupture in their relationship has been emotionally disabling for Jan. His difference resides in the fact that he is a blond Japanese, and since his father lives out a fantasy life based on the twelfth-century court of Lady Murasaki, such a difference is completely unacceptable. He chose the genetic material for his son from that of another Murasaki: although she was both an explorer and architect he chose her purely for her name, not noticing that her own genetic inheritance was both Japanese and Dutch. McIntyre uses Jan's mixed genetic inheritance to suggest that cultural fantasies are implicated in the desire to exclude difference, particularly where race is concerned, although this is not developed in the narrative.

The psychic and emotional completion of each of the characters is prevented by the way in which identity is defined within the binary oppositions of sameness and difference, self and other, and a central interest of the narrative is the conditions of existence of the fractured selves which result from those dualisms. In its articulation of the 'spatial experience' of fragmentation and dislocation, the narrative is concerned to extricate difference from the unequal power relations within which it is embedded. The experience of fragmentation and dislocation that is invoked by the title of the book is also expressed by means of the conflicts between inside and outside, sameness and difference that are scattered throughout the narrative. At one stage in the narrative, Mischa intrudes into the symbolic heart of the Centre, the Stone Palace, in the vain hope of persuading the head of the ruling family that controls the space port to give her work on one of his space ships. Her punishment for this incursion is to be placed in an artificial skin which is a sophisticated kind of sensory-deprivation device:

> Disorientation caught Mischa and shook her. Her eyes were closed and she could not open them. The darkness was the scarlet of her body heat, veined with the images of capillaries in her eyelids, holding nothing but fog beyond. She floated in an environment that lacked gravity, pressure, and light, surrounded by something that soaked up everything she could see or hear or touch or smell. She tried to move, and it seemed she might be able to, in slow, slow motion, through an amorphous, yielding substance, but she strained her arm against it until the muscles ached, and when she finally relaxed she was in the same position from which she had started. (33)

Her total enclosure within this device serves as an appropriate metaphor for the confining and coercive environment of the Centre, but it also suggests the experience of depthlessness and dislocation that Jameson notes as one of the key conditions of postmodernism. Although he tends to see this spatial experience negatively, or at least as unmapped territory, there is a strong indication in McIntyre's narrative that such dislocation can enable alternative forms of identity and subjectivity to emerge. The motif of 'exile' which runs through the narrative suggests that only those who are outside the prevailing rules and structures are likely to establish such alternatives.

Both dislocation and disorientation are presented as necessary stages in the development of oppositional spatial and psychic environments within which social and sexual relations can be re-imagined. In this context, the dislocation and disturbance that Subtwo experiences in his struggle to achieve emotional and psychic distance from his pseudo-sib can be regarded as part of the process by which such alternative environments are developed. The difference in the effect that the Centre has on the pseudo-sibs hastens their separation. The disorderly environment of the Stone Palace furthers the moral degeneration of Subone but causes extreme mental dislocation in Subtwo:

The passages continued on and on, until Subtwo felt their irregularities affecting him. His balance began to falter. He liked level floors and right angles; this was a place of bumps and projections and random curves. At first he sensed the same reaction from his pseudosib, and he was comforted that he was not, at least, alone, but they progressed and Subone's discomfort decreased as his interest rose. Subtwo was upset and wished again that the lock between them would complete its dissolution. (46)

Although he and Subone are not twins, their reactions have been linked experimentally in such a way that they are the 'behavioural equivalents of genetic twins'. Their programming has resulted in an artificial convergence of their personalities and needs, at the expense of the real differences between them. The recovery of those differences is made indispensable in terms of the narrative, because Subtwo is the means by which Mischa eventually leaves Earth. The assertion of difference and the dissolution of the link with Subone enables Subtwo to begin to form a genuine emotional attachment to someone else, appropriately enough with one of the Centre's former slaves.

Jan is presented as being so passive and inert that he is virtually disabled by the Oedipal conflict with his father. This conflict is mediated through technology, in that Jan, like the pseudo-sibs, is the product of reproductive technology, having been reproduced from the genetic material of a woman long dead. Even here his father exerts absolute authority, since he chose the genetic material from which Jan would be reproduced. It is Mischa who articulates the common elements in the Oedipal narratives of control and conflict, exhibited in the structures of the Centre and in Jan's relationship with his father:

> She sounded shocked, and a little angry. 'Is the Sphere just like Centre? Do they play with each other's lives too?'
> 'No' – Jan hesitated. No one had ever expressed his own questions in those words and those sentiments. He did not like the idea of himself as a complicated plaything, though he had long before accepted that his father would always try to direct his life in ways that ordinary families would not. 'Yes, I guess they do, to a certain extent. People always do.' (107)

His contact with Mischa allows him to counteract his sense of himself as a superfluous 'plaything' and provides him with something to which he can commit himself. When the pseudo-sibs have taken over the Stone Palace, Mischa returns there to see if she can persuade them to take her and her brother off-world. She interests Subtwo enough for him to assign Jan to be her teacher. However, Subone's increasing desire for the domination that stems from the imposition of pain and fear results in his fatal wounding of Mischa's brother, and in retaliation he is himself wounded by Mischa. Mischa and Jan have to take to the underground to escape from the revenge that Subtwo feels emotionally obliged to attain for his wounded sib.

The journey to the underworld proves, not unexpectedly, to be one of redemption, and the underground city's own underground is clearly a symbolically significant space in the narrative: it is the place to which all the radiation-affected mutants from the Centre are exiled, to become truly marginal and other. The depiction of this space suggests that the story is, more than anything else, a narrative of domination and subordination based on the eradication of difference. The response of the mutants to their exile has been to choose to live by different rules from the Centre, to care for those who are helpless and to establish a different kind of collectivity. This is no utopia, however, and the knowledge of the underground community that is provided by the narrative is very sketchy. Interestingly enough, they are reluctant to accept Jan amongst them because he has no mutation, which again underlines the central question of difference. They emerge from the underground at the end of the novel and challenge the spatial and cultural boundaries imposed on them by returning to the city, apparently not to overthrow the ruling families but simply to insist on their right to be there, and to have their difference recognised.

To remain with the spatial metaphor, the potential for development of those who have chosen to cross the social and psychic boundaries implied by the notion of 'exile' is validated by the narrative. Thus, the mutants leave their underground exile and Subtwo, Jan and Mischa leave Earth. However, the Sphere worlds for which they have left the Centre are not presented as any kind of utopian alternative, any more than the underground was, as the veiled textual references to the manipulative lifestyles and politics practised in the Sphere are intended to show. Whether or not the return of the Centre's repressed, in the form of its mutant others, is intended to make any difference to the existing power structures is not made clear.

While these incomplete scenarios are undoubtedly part of the novel's ambiguous response to the difficult question of cultural transformation and social change, the open-ended narrative is also a refusal to subscribe to the generic demands of science fiction narratives for some kind of conservative recuperation. The political unconscious of the narrative is also that of the 1970s, in which a libertarian suspicion of centralised agency of any kind leads to a belief that change which takes place at the margins has more validity because of its apparent spontaneity. Attempts in the narrative to establish new paradigms for social and sexual relations are extremely tentative, and at the end of the novel, the characters remain dispersed and fragmented, about to pursue deliberately diverse aims and ambitions. Whatever collective responses were activated in the narrative remain temporary and peripheral, and what unity there is between them comes from the fact that they have all been subject to, and have resisted, the repressive desire to exclude difference and to restore sameness. As the boundaries between centre and margins, inside and outside, become unstable, the notion of 'exile' becomes increasingly contradictory, and as such it is indicative of the impossibility of closure in the narrative.

The instability of the boundary between insider and outsider suggested by the spatial metaphor can also be seen in *Dreamsnake*, which is McIntyre's second novel. The closed-off and static space of the Centre is a more shadowy presence in the narrative, although it is made clear that, from the perspective of those ruling the Centre, the outside and those who live in it remain threatening in their difference. However, as the preferential relationship between outside and inside, centre and margins, is effectively reversed in the narrative, this perspective is given little credibility. The outside is celebrated as fragmented, open and evolving, as are the new forms of social and sexual relations developing there.

Gender relations are explored more directly than in *The Exile Waiting*, particularly through the narrative concern with female desire. Although the narrative follows the science fiction convention of the post-holocaust society in which a quest is undertaken by a strong central character, the emphasis on male desire which is found in such conventions is undermined here. Because gender relations are re-examined from a feminist perspective, and because the central character is female, the post-holocaust landscape provides a spacial and textual environment for the inscription of female desire in the narrative. The central character is a healer called Snake, and her travels through the post-holocaust world bring her into contact with variously constructed social groupings which inhabit the landscape. In keeping with the feminist perspective offered by the text, the communities themselves are depicted as self-sufficient and decentralised, and the prioritising of female desire in the narrative allows the representation of the different communities to foreground gender relations.

Snake is so named because she heals using the poison from the fangs of snakes, and like all healers, she has developed immunity to their poison. In a playful reversal of the biblical myth, not only is the post-holocaust world depicted as having more utopian possibilites than the very un-edenic Centre, but woman is in control of the serpents, not the other way round. The patriarchal expulsion from the garden into the wilderness becomes the precondition for the formation of new and different versions of gender relations, rather than a source of existential despair. The narrative concerns the loss of Snake's dreamsnake while she is healing a young boy in a small desert community. She underestimates the fear of snakes that would exist within such a community, and is unable to prevent one of the boy's terrified parents from killing the dreamsnake. The signifance of the dreamsnake is that it is a rare alien species which is essential to healers because its bite brings relief from pain. Efforts by the healers to clone dreamsnakes have met with little success and so both Snake and the desert community feel guilt at a loss which could have been avoided if they had had more understanding of one another.

The narrative focuses primarily on Snake's attempt to find another dreamsnake, and although there is also an emergent relationship between Snake and Arevin, a man from the desert community, it is left relatively undeveloped. Snake initially goes to the Centre to try to obtain another dreamsnake, but appropriately enough she finally finds an entire colony of them outside, in a wrecked alien dome. The shifting of narrative precedence from inside to outside and the different forms of otherness that this incorporates is made explicit when Snake reaches the Centre. For Snake, the Centre is the mysterious other; to the Centre, Snake is a fearful other from the outside and all that the 'outside' represents. The response of the Family representative who listens to her request for another dreamsnake, or access to the technology that would permit successful cloning, clearly demonstrates this: 'Genetic manipulation – Gods, we have enough trouble with mutation without inducing it deliberately! You're lucky I couldn't let you in, healer. I'd have to denounce you. You'd spend your life in exile with the rest of the freaks.'[9] In the outside, genetic manipulation is used for healing: in the Centre, it is feared as a source of increasing mutation. The moral judgement in the narrative is explicit and confirms the outside as the place in which regeneration is possible in both individual and social terms; the Centre, on the other hand, signifies those discourses of authority which the narrative itself is concerned to disrupt.

Dreamsnake contains a significant rewriting of the convention of the heroic quest from a gendered perspective: Snake's position as the main character enables gender to become central to the narrative, and this is reinforced within the narrative through the social and cultural authority that she acquires as a healer. The quest for the dreamsnake is an opportunity to explore gender relations by means of the differently structured communities that Snake encounters. In the desert communities, the group leaders are women and individuals partner together in threes, two male and one female. The description of such partnerings is the closest that McIntyre comes to suggesting an alternative to heterosexuality, although its significance is downplayed in the narrative as a whole. Men are active in childcare, and sexual pleasure is inseparable from bio-control of personal fertility, a narrative strategy that enables McIntyre to criticise obliquely the power relations inherent in reproductive technology. The mountain communities are described as more closed and patriarchal, and it is from one of these communities that Snake adopts an abused child, Melissa, who, as both her daughter and friend, accompanies her on the search for the dreamsnake. All the communities are shown to be in various stages of change and development, and there is none of the absolute resistance to change shown by the Centre; family structures outside the Centre are open and extended in deliberate contrast to the oppressively hierarchical structures implied by the Centre.

The emphasis on alternative forms of social and sexual relations is reinforced through the motif of the dreamsnakes: when Snake finds the dreamsnakes she discovers that the reason the healers had so little success in breeding the snakes was because they assumed that they bred in twos, when in fact they breed in threes:

Dreamsnakes were triploid, and they required a triplet, not a pair. Snake's mental laughter faded away into a sad smile of regret for all the mistakes she and her people had made for so many years, hampered as they were by lack of the proper information, by a mechanical technology insufficient to support the biological possibilities, by ethnocentrism. And by the forced isolation of earth from other worlds, by the self imposed isolation of too many groups of people from each other. (266)

This is a fairly clear declaration of the interests of the narrative in the kind of change and renewal that can come about through the acceptance of difference. The strange and inexplicably shattered alien dome in which the dreamsnakes are breeding is an appropriate spatial representation for the kinds of reversals that the novel has been attempting:

> The strangeness of the place hit Snake like a physical blow. Alien plants grew all around the base of the tremendous half-collapsed structure, nearly to the cliff, leaving no clear path at all. What covered the ground resembled nothing Snake knew, not grass or scrub or bushes. It was a flat borderless expanse of bright red leaf. (234)

Snake's discovery challenges the kinds of closures represented by all binary oppositions, a challenge that has already been suggested both by the narrative emphasis on new kinds of communities and relationships, and by McIntyre's use of the quest convention. Snake's search for the dreamsnake takes precedence in the narrative over Arevin's search for her. He initiates little in the narrative, his role is simply to retrace her journey until he finds her, and he arrives when she has already found the dreamsnakes.

The narrative ends at that point, with all the relationships largely unresolved and incomplete, but redolent with possibilities. That such irresolution can seem positive and optimistic would seem to endorse Jameson's comment that our reading of SF narratives is directed away from an interest in linear causality and towards the spatial environment itself. The spacial heterogeneity within these narratives provides an environment in which alternative gender relations can be explored. However, despite their open-endedness, the narratives cannot entirely eradicate the presence of the hierarchical and centralised structures of power represented by the ubiquitous Centre. Although repressed in the text, the power structures suggested by the Centre are precisely those that are deeply embedded in our social and psychic relations, and their presence induces ambiguity and incompleteness in any narrative attempt to envision new sets of relations. At the same time, however, the irresolution of the narratives is also a means of contesting the totalising nature of the dominant representations.

The rewriting of SF conventions to prioritise female desire and the destabilising effect that this has on representations of gender can be seen clearly in McIntyre's later novel, *Superluminal*. This is not a post-holocaust novel; instead it assumes that the colonisation of space has long since taken place. The relationship between earth and the colony planets is not presented as an issue, but the narrative hints that the economies of those worlds depend on exporting luxury goods to an Earth which has become a non-manufacturing consumer society with a service economy. *Superluminal* is our own post-industrial future present. Much of the interest in the novel lies in the way that it draws on conventions from other popular narratives in order to interrogate representations of gender, in particular those of romance fiction. Romance fiction constructs a desiring female subject and identification with that subject is part of the pleasure offered to readers of romance. The narrative of *Superluminal* oscillates between the poles of representation familiar to romance and those familiar to science fiction, and the overlapping subject positions offered to the reader have the effect of disrupting expected narrative pleasures.

The narrative not only focuses unexpectedly on emotional and psychic experiences but it also revolves, directly and indirectly, around the passionate love affair between the two central characters, Laenea Trevelyan and Radu Dracul. McIntyre here moves out of conventional science fiction territory and explicitly borrows from the conventions of a different generic form, that of romance fiction. The dislocations that structured the spatial experience of McIntyre's earlier novels are now developed in the context of romance themes, and the contradictory elements of the narrative undermine the assumptions about gender identity that are built into the conventions of both science fiction and romance.

The opening sentence of the novel, 'She gave up her heart quite willingly', is one that would be equally at home in romance fiction, and the phrase is meant both literally and metaphorically in the narrative. It refers to the biotechnological solution to the problem of travel between dimensions, as well as to the love affair between the two central characters. In order to avoid the neccessity of being

totally anaesthetised for travel at faster-than-light speed, the pilots
of ships travelling at such speeds accept the replacement of their own
biologically inadequate hearts by a microelectronic device of stagger-
ing sophistication. Soon after Laenea has undergone the transplant,
she meetes Radu. The ironic mixture of future technology and
romantic involvement is deliberately unsettling: because the position
of key characters is not fixed within the conventions of either
romance or science fiction, generic boundaries become unstable and
the text is able to adopt a critical position towards genre conventions
and the assumptions they contain.

Boundaries between nature and culture are also destabilised as
the main groups of characters have all undergone some genetic or
technological alteration, resulting in the blurring of the boundaries
between human and machine. Orca is a diver whose people have
chosen genetic alteration in order to survive the deep-sea conditions
that will enable them to communicate and live in harmony with
ceteceans. Orca describes them as 'more different than a race, but
less different than a separate species. We're a transition phase'.[10]
Radu Dracul survives a virus that alters his, and potentially all,
human perception, of the relation between space and time. They
become, in effect, the 'cyborgs' proposed by Donna Haraway, who
'make very problematic the statuses of man or woman, human,
artefact, member of a race, individual identity, or body'.[11]

The emphasis on difference, and the fluidity of genre and gender
boundaries, suggests a textual focus on the social and cultural
constructions of identity. The affair between Laenea and Radu ends
because her cyborg status means that her biorhythms are no longer
compatible with those of ordinary humans. This becomes clear when
both she and Radu experience increasingly violent and uncontroll-
able orgasms which become life-threatening for them. This has, of
course, to be seen ironically in terms of romance conventions, but in
SF terms it is explained by a reference to the technology:

> Her system and that of any normal human being would no longer
> mesh. The change in her was too disturbing, on psychological and
> subliminal levels, while normal biorhythms were so compelling that
> they interfered with and would eventually destroy her new biological
> integrity. (62)

Laenea's ambition to be a pilot and her artificial heart have set her
free from both biological and social constraints.

McIntyre brings the generic conventions and the subjectivities constructed by the different kinds of narrative into playful and ironic collision here. In a text marked by female desire, Laenea emerges as a strong central character because she has exceeded the social and cultural determinants of gender and identity that are built into the genre conventions of both SF and romance, and much the same is true of Orca the diver. Nor can Radu's character be described in terms of the conventions of narratives usually associated with male desire: he is not given to excesses of heroic violence, he is surprisingly dependent on the female characters, and often cries in the narrative. The story does involve him in Laenea's rescue when her ship is lost in the hitherto undiscovered seventh dimension, but he finds her through the psychic link that develops between them rather than through any traditional heroics.

The spatial experience of disorientation and dislocation in the novel facilitates an exploration of the boundaries of gender and identity in a number of interesting ways. The altered states of the central female characters in the novel alert us to the fact that social and cultural categorisations are being radically questioned. Laenea's decision to step outside the confines of ordinary human existence by becoming a pilot is endorsed by the fact that on her first flight she discovers the seventh dimension: although all the pilots are able to think spatially in as many as four dimensions, even the most experienced had been unable to find the almost mythical seventh dimension. Although Radu is able to find her through their psychic link, he remains physically unable to become a pilot and so they remain physically incompatible. But his psychic abilities enable him to communicate with the giant ceteceans that the divers live amongst, and so, with the possibility of genetic alteration enabling him to become a diver, he, too, is in transition from one state to another. These altered human states are to do with excess and transgression, with the crossing of gender and identity boundaries as well as generic boundaries, and with the celebration of difference.

The presence of other boundaries in the text that are to do with relations of domination are signified by the post-industrial, post-colonial environment of *Superluminal*, which is presented as being both liberatory and repressive in the same way that the Administration is both benign and intolerant. The narrative raises the politics of difference by posing different forms of identity and collectivity against one another. The divers, for example, represent a community at odds with the Administration, specifically with the government of the United States, since their identification with the ceteceans involved an apparently unfinished war with that administration which made them 'traitors' in the eyes of the US government. The pilots are an elite group that is both used by and also uses the Administration: their value lies in the technological investment that they represent and in the increased profitability that results from the rapid transportation of luxury goods from the colonies to Earth. The narrative suggests that the technology itself is sustained by the exploitative political and economic relationship that exists between Earth and the colonised planets and although this is never fully articulated, it persists as an undercurrent in the narrative. These structures, and the power relations that are implicit in them, represent the borders beyond which the numerous 'others' in the text strive to go. The incorporation of conventions from romance into science fiction undermines generic differences, as well as those between nature and culture, self and other, and as boundaries become increasingly unstable, closure around such differences becomes impossible.

Not surprisingly, these contradictions appear clearly in McIntyre's 'Star Trek' novel *The Entropy Effect* (1981; 1988) in which the boundaries of space and time are stretched to allow the death and 'rebirth' of Captain Kirk. The hierarchical and colonialising power structure signified by references to Starbase and Starfleet, and enacted on the Starship *Enterprise*, are fundamentally unquestioned in political terms, but the pathology of power which they represent is challenged by the representations of gender in the novel. The toppling of the figure of the father, albeit as a temporary measure, is enough to allow the possibility of alternative scenarios to emerge. Indeed, the story is about alternative scenarios created by the discovery by physicist Dr Mordreaux of bioelectronic crystals which allow people to travel back in time.

Time travel induces changes in time itself, and the different time tracks split into multiple and disintegrating lines, which begin the process of entropy in the universe. It is in one of these time tracks that Kirk is killed by Dr Mordreaux, just as he is about to admit to a treasured friend and former lover his own past failings in their relationship. His former lover is also the captain of a starship and member of a family of nine partners. It was the non-nuclear and non-hierarchical family and partnership structure that Kirk found unacceptable, as would be expected from such a patriarchal figure, and which precipitated the end of their relationship. He is, of course, restored to life by the elimination of that time track and the destruction of the crystals that allowed time travel.

By experimenting with the possibility of Kirk's elimination from the narrative, the fixed nature of the power relations signified by all Starfleet references is temporarily called into question, and Kirk as the sign of the invincible father is removed. When he is returned to temporal normality, he is unaware of his earlier death, and the reader is thus implicated in the undermining of Kirk's apparently unassailable position as patriarch. In addition, the relationships that have been foregrounded by the narrative do not return to the same state, and Kirk unaccountably makes several small changes to improve the situation of several crew members, as well as making the decision to contact his former lover to effect some kind of reconciliation.

The final entry in the 'Captain's Log', functioning as a suitably masculine version of 'Dear Diary', becomes an ironic device for indicating the limitations of patriarchal ideology, since the way Kirk reports those decisions shows his own limited knowledge of events; Spock, on the other hand, as always in his role as Kirk's desiring other, has a complete knowledge of those events which he declines to share with Kirk:

> My science officer shows no more sign than before that he is willing to discuss the 'unpredictable events' that occurred during his observations. Despite a certain temptation to ask him if this is information that we were not meant to know – a question that would undoubtedly grate upon his scientific objectivity – I'm not inclined to press him for more answers. It's possible that he simply made some sort of mistake that would humiliate him to reveal.[12]

Because of the gaps in his knowledge, Kirk is not wholly restored to a position of authority in the narrative, and although the hierarchical relations of the Starship are also restored, they are not entirely the same as they were.[13] Spock is established as the holder of knowledge, and therefore authority, but as Kirk's other, he is not in a position to exert that authority. The contradiction between the appearance and the actuality of the power structures of the starship cannot be resolved in favour of the alien other. The familiar conventions of time travel and the possibility of alternative realities allows the narrative to resist closure around unquestioned assumptions of inequality in gender relations. The use of familiar conventions in McIntyre's other work has produced similarly open-ended narratives, in which contradictions around gender in particular seem unresolvable. If the spatial experience of postmodernity is disturbing, it is at least partly due to the way in which such irresolution reveals the presence of gender relations.

Disruption and Discontinuity in the Narratives of C.J. Cherryh

The novels of C.J. Cherryh are, on one level, highly conventional SF narratives, except for the fact that they are full of women characters who occupy the familiar roles of battlefleet commanders, space pilots, soldiers and so on. Since there is no recourse to narrative devices which might suggest that these are socially and sexually unacceptable roles for women, the narratives are able to go some way towards reconstructing the terms in which gender relations are usually presented in SF. Although the generic conventions do not allow Cherryh to go very far in her reconstruction of gender identity and gender relations, the narratives challenge the limits and constraints of the dominant representations. The tension between the familiar narrative framework and the unfamiliar representation of gender results in open-ended narratives in which the relationship between gender and genre has become unstable. Cherryh's narratives exploit this instability, and despite their conventional appearance, they disrupt conventional definitions of difference and otherness.

The narratives are complex and dense, and often involve cultural and social dislocation on a massive temporal and spatial scale. Such massive dislocation and lack of fixity provides the framework within which the revisioning of gender relations can take place. The Downbelow novels, for example, are set in a universe in which two main blocs of relatively fixed political and economic interests compete for the control of vast areas of space. Since these interests, known as Union and Alliance, are characterised by their similarity, the narratives can focus on what is of difference to them. The question of difference, of what it means to be alien and outside, is a central concern in Cherryh's novels. What happens at the peripheries of these vast spatial territories is presented as being more significant than events at the centre. Cherryh has written a number of novels in which the inter-relationship between human and alien species is examined, and the difficulties involved in the development of some kind of understanding of, and respect for, difference is the main interest of these narratives.

The concepts of reproductive technology and genetic engineering are often used in the novels to invoke the ambiguities inherent in the distinction between sameness and difference, and, since it has possibilities for either domination and liberation, the technology provides an appropriate metaphor through which to convey those ambiguities. In the Downbelow novels, it is explicitly linked to aggressive colonisation, as Union laboratories produce whole generations of a genetically engineered underclass of people known as the 'azi'. Azi learn a single task, whether it is childcare or soldiering, and they are used as raw material in wars or on newly colonised planets. The relationship between those who are 'lab born' and those who are born from a human parent is as central to the question of establishing the importance of difference as is the relationship between humans and other species.

The novel *Forty Thousand in Gehenna* (1983; 1986) combines alien and genetically engineered differences by setting the novel on a planet colonised by Union forces, which is then abandoned by the administrative centre for political reasons. The colonising population consists of forty thousand of the genetically engineered azi, with a few human supervisors. In the conditions which begin to prevail once it is clear that no more supply ships will be arriving, these distinctions begin to break down. Added to this, there is an indigenous and intelligent population that the colonists call 'calibans' to signify both their reptilian appearance and the threat of difference that they represent. The calibans begin to disrupt and eventually to destroy the settlements, forcing the people out of their enclosed environment and into the landscape inhabited by the calibans. The changes that result from the collapse of barriers between the human and non-human inhabitants of the planet, as well as those between the azi and the humans, are considered on a timescale of hundreds of years. The narrative details the interaction between the human descendants of the original 'lab born' population and the calibans, and describes a new and developing social and cultural environment in which previous distinctions to do with gender and culture have become meaningless.

When Gehenna is finally revisited, it is by representatives from the Alliance power bloc which, in the course of its war with the Union, has forced the Union to cede to it Gehenna and other planets. The reactions of the bewildered observers are used as a device to describe the complex and different culture which has developed through the interaction and integration of two intelligent but wholly different species, and, as one of the first observers comments, 'We are ironically faced with a first-contact situation involving our own species.'[14] It is the absence of the absolute distinction between human and other that the outside observers find impossible to understand, particularly since they bring their own sets of precise distinctions with them, which include gender distinctions.

The conflict in the narrative between the conceptual framework of the observers and the actual developments on Gehenna indicates that the narrative is concerned to redefine boundaries between nature and culture, and alien and other. The evolving relationships on Gehenna can no longer be fixed within those boundaries, since they provide evidence of 'the intrusion of one genetic inheritance upon another across the boundaries of hitherto uncrossable space' (199). The appropriated narrative conventions of SF are used here to question the basis of the 'hitherto uncrossable' space created by the tension between sameness and difference, and the gendered nature of this space is explored in the narrative as the team of observers, sent to study the developing culture on Gehenna, splits along gender lines. The male observer, Genley, joins the group of Gehennans which is male-led, hierarchical and territorially aggressive, while Elizabeth McGee joins the other group, which is more defensive and female-led.

In an equally crucial distinction between the observers, Genley fails to see events in anything other than human terms and helps to provoke war between the two groups by breaking the rule of non-interference and providing advanced technology. In contrast, Elizabeth McGee struggles to understand the nature of the events from a Gehennan point of view, which is utterly different from anything she has encountered elsewhere. This willingness to accommodate difference is endorsed in the narrative when the forces with which Genley identified himself are defeated, and he is killed. At the conclusion of the narrative, the view is expressed that 'A Gehennan sees things a different way' (445), which constitutes a recognition that Gehennan society and culture is too complex to fit into a binary definition of difference. Because of their close alliance with humans, the non-human presence and perception of the calibans are presented in the narrative as different but not other. The relationship between the human and the alien on Gehenna produces an account of difference that works against the oppositional relations between masculine and feminine, self and other that are implicit in the SF convention of the alien.

The spacial and temporal dislocation referred to in the narrative is both interplanetary and planetary, and takes place across many generations. Indeed, the timescale is so stretched out that it becomes almost meaningless in terms of a conventional sense of linear causality, and this enables the focus of the narrative to remain with the 'spatial experience', as Jameson put it. This makes it possible for a seemingly conventional science fiction narrative to confront culturally determined attitudes towards both racial and sexual difference. It is Cherryh's appropriation of the generic conventions that enables her to explore these themes persistently within her work, using the possibilities provided by the spacial and temporal dimensions of the genre to break down the boundaries between what is and what could be, and undermining fixed notions of sameness and difference.

In order to explore the extent to which definitions of difference are culturally determined, Cherryh makes a more radical use of the convention of the alien in several novels, by placing the non-human and female at the centre of the narrative, and the recognisably human and male at the periphery. In the *Chanur's Pride* series, the central characters are not only all female but they are also members of a non-human race, the Hani. They have claws, fur, beards and manes, and are captain and crew of the ship *Chanur's Pride* because, ironically, the males of the species are too temperamentally unstable to go into space. The crew of each ship is made up of the members of an extended family group, the female head of which becomes the ship's captain.

The trilogy develops a narrative which concerns inter-species politics in the borderless territories of deep space, and those already unstable politics are made more complex by the incursion of humans into the territories. In the first novel of the series, *The Pride of Chanur* (1981; 1983), the first humans to venture into alien space are captured by the Kif, one of the alien species, and the only survivor of that capture is Tully, who escapes from his captors onto the Hani ship. He is therefore positioned as doubly alien, not only because he is human but also because he is male. Because the narrative represents the male as both alien and outsider, he is rendered powerless. Contrary to the expectations generated by the otherwise conventional narrative, Tully does not assert himself to take on more heroic proportions. He remains a powerless alien, totally dependent on the care of others for his wellbeing. The perspective offered by the narrative is both disconcerting and disruptive for readers of conventional SF texts. The male character remains a shadowy figure, and the convention of the alien is used to shift the focus of the narrative towards an examination of gender relations, and of the way in which difference is socially and culturally determined.

In the end, however, Tully is restored to a slightly more central position by the appearance of more humans in Hani space, amongst whom he clearly has some standing. At the same time, the humans are still seen as the alien species, which means that the relations of difference continue to trouble the narrative. At the conclusion of the trilogy, Tully has become something of an outsider to his own species, and he therefore chooses to stay with the Hani as a subordinate and alien male, rather than go with the humans, where, by implication, the relations of power are more familiarly in the patriarchal mould. Although the narrative does not sustain a radical repositioning of masculinity, the complete restoration of the dominant relations of power is prevented. The interesting but covert suggestion of inter-species sex between Tully and one of the ship's female crew, although it is glossed over, creates another troubling moment in the narrative around the issue of sexuality. Although Cherryh rarely disputes the dominance of heterosexuality, recognition of other possibilities is implicit in the unexplored notion of cross-species sex. While the conventional narrative structure undoubtedly restricts the extent to which gender and difference can be rethought, the areas of irresolution in the narrative prevent it from closing down around the binary oppositions which structure the dominant power relations.

The limitations of the conventional SF structures within which Cherryh works can be clearly seen in relation to the presentation of technology, specifically reproductive technology, which is neither closely examined nor celebrated in the narratives. Cherryh's focus tends to be more on the kinds of social and cultural relations which develop in the context of the spaces that have become available as a result of technology. Her narratives are often concerned with power politics on a huge scale, but since it is the minute individual responses to those politics that are the focus of the narratives, the power politics, like the technology, tend to be taken for granted. So the restructuring of gender relations and the important questioning of both racial and sexual stereotypes that goes on in the narratives has to be weighed against the fact that the narratives do not, on the whole, attempt to question the wider social and political environment. The spacial and temporal dislocation in the narratives that is crucial for the formulation of alternative social and sexual relations, is also restrictive, in that it effaces the actual politics of technological domination and colonisation.

The two power blocs of Union and Alliance that feature in the Downbelow and Merchanter novels illustrate this. Alliance is a loose grouping of merchant ships, some of which are so huge that they contain thousands of people, all of whom are members of the ship's 'family'. The families are matrilineal in that the children are conceived outside the ships, in deliberately casual stopovers in space ports, to ensure both genetic diversity and non-patriarchal relations. The ships themselves provide the environment in which women have absolute equality with men. Alliance forces are not located on worlds but in space, and as the term 'alliance' suggests, they are not structured around hierarchies. Union forces, on the other hand, are a grouping of worlds which rebelled against the domination of Earth, and became colonisers themselves, using genetic engineering to create their armies.

The genetically engineered azi are the dark side of technology, they are considered to be second-class citizens whose sole function is to serve, and as such they are both oppressors and oppressed. Although the uses to which the reproductive technology is put are seen in this context as repressive rather than emancipatory, the technology itself is not questioned. By suggesting that the technology is benign, Cherryh ignores the inter-relation between technology and power, and indeed that is never foregrounded in the novels. However, in terms of race and gender, that relationship is a crucial one. The opposition between the two power blocs provides the background rather than the motivation for the narratives, which accounts in part for the tension between the restructured social and sexual relations and the unrestructured political environment.

A later novel by Cherryh, *Cyteen* (1988), also issued as a trilogy,

is set in the Merchanter's universe and demonstrates this contradiction quite clearly. The first novel in the trilogy, *Cyteen: The betrayal*
(1988; February 1989), is set in Reseune on Cyteen Station, the
centre of Union's genetic engineering industrial complex. The key
character in the novel is Ariane Emory, a woman of immense power
who controls an industrial and military complex that spans whole
planets. These are the only novels by Cherryh in which the question
of reproductive technology and its effect on sexual relations is
explored in some detail. Cloning from original genetic material has
produced a situation in which the universe is populated by the
genetic offspring of so many people that the whole idea of the nuclear
family has become meaningless:

> She was anomalous, child of two parents, Olga Emory and James
> Carnath. They had founded the labs at Reseune, had begun the
> process that had shaped Union itself. They had sent out the colonists,
> the soldiers. Their own genes had gone into hundreds of them. Her
> quasi-relatives were scattered across lightyears. But so were every-
> one's, these days. In her lifetime even that basic human thinking had
> changed; biological parentage was a trivial connection. Family
> mattered, the larger, the more extended . . . the safer and more
> prosperous.[15]

Cloning has made it possible for a child to be created which is the
exact replica of its parent. The technology has produced a situation
in which the self can be endlessly fragmented by being 'scattered
across lightyears', but at the same time that self can be exactly
reproduced by means of memory banks.

The creation of multiple selves is both liberatory and repressive,
particularly where gender is concerned, and the narrative reflects
that uncertainty. In an environment such as this, Oedipal relations
and their accompanying hierarchies are undermined and yet
reproduced through the medium of designer genetics. As in other
Cherryh novels, the existing political structure remains intact, since
this is not a work about the politics of planetary or interplanetary
revolution; the concern with genetic engineering provides a way into
discussion of sexual relations, and, for virtually the first time in her
novels, non-heterosexual relations. It is as if a focus on the
technology of reproduction has created a space hitherto unavailable
in Cherryh's narratives, in which discussion of sex and gender is
acceptable in narrative terms.

Although *Cyteen: The betrayal* focuses on Ariane Emory's

genetic work and her desire to replicate intelligence through psychogenesis, it also details the way she uses her power to set up a series of masochistic sexual encounters with Justin, an adolescent boy who is psychically damaged by the whole encounter. The repressive power relations reproduce those common to many SF narratives with a male protagonist. Ariane is subsequently murdered and the rest of the trilogy concerns the generation, childhood and adolescence of Ariane's clone, who is to carry on her work. The narrative framework imposes constraints on the extent to which the relationship between sexuality and power can be explored, however, and the possibility that Ariane's murder might have had a sexual motive is finally dismissed by the suggestion that Ariane's death was the result of political rather than sexual motivation. Despite attempts to bury them, however, sexual relations *do* continue to appear in the texts. In the years following her death, Justin, the boy who was subjected to Ariane's desire, has devastating flashbacks to his experience with her. Although they are intended to have a distancing effect, the flashbacks are so vivid that they alter the narrative's desired focus. The solving of the murder and the minutiae of Reseune politics are actually less important than the continued discussion of sexual relations through the technique of flashback, although their function is clearly to repress the concern with sexuality. Both Justin and the cloned Ariane turn to azi lovers, but Justin's choice of a male lover is complicated by the fact that it is his own father's genetic material from which his lover has been reproduced.

The narrative becomes confused about its direction and oscillates between being conventional science fiction and attempting, with limited success, a much more ambitious re-examination of the relations of dominance, both technological and sexual. Gwyneth Jones has described it as 'a novel about inner space, not outer space, spiralling in ever decreasing circles around the bunker of the undead dictator: an experience as claustrophobic, as disorientating, as remorseless as about two years in a sensory deprivation tank'.[16] Cherryh finally, and disappointingly, steps back from the possibilities hinted at in the narrative for other definitions of identity and difference, and for other kinds of sexual and social relations. Probably those possibilities could not, in the end, be realised within a conventional science fiction narrative.

The trilogy remains a disorientating experience, however,

because even though both gender and identity are mediated through a largely unquestioned technology, they become detached from their fixed positions during the course of the narrative. Despite a conventional and unsatisfying dénouement couched in terms of a somewhat traditional power struggle which Ariane's clone, Ari, wins, the uncertainty generated by unresolved questions about sexual and power relations is not entirely contained by the narrative structure. The possibilities for new forms of social and sexual relations that are opened up by the technology of reproduction are not intended to become the focus of the narrative, but the conventional structure is so disrupted by the failure of the narrative to resolve the complex issues which it has raised that that is exactly what happens. The central characters in the trilogy are all marked by their genetically engineered otherness as far as patriarchal familial relations are concerned; they repeatedly transgress the boundaries between sameness and difference and prevent closure around such distinctions. The contradictions that are inherent in such transgressions cannot be resolved within the conventional narrative structure, which is why it remains both fragmented and open-ended.

Chapter 4

Troubles in Women's Country

Separatist Female Futures in Feminist SF

A favourite science fiction convention is that of the disaster, some cataclysmic event that has profound consequences for human society. This is a useful convention for allowing the social tensions and fears of the present to be extrapolated in a fairly direct way into the future. In the books discussed in this chapter the convention has been rewritten in such a way that responsibility for the cataclysm is ascribed wholly to patriarchy, and, in effect, patriarchy itself is presented as the disaster. The definition of woman as alien and other is effectively reversed in the women-only communities of the ensuing post-holocaust world, in order to provide a critique of gender relations.

At the same time, however, the disaster convention has certain resonances that are hard to ignore. Because they extrapolate from the present to the future in such a direct way, disaster novels tend to be exceedingly deterministic. The range of anxieties about technology and social processes that are reproduced in the texts are tied to a view of social and sexual relations that is largely based on a notion of fixed and unchanging gender identities. The attempt to reconstitute gender relations through appropriation of this particular convention and its re-use as a vehicle for the production of women-centred narratives is, therefore, a difficult undertaking. The female communities that are depicted do not so much problematise gender relations as reproduce them, so that the communities themselves are based on relations of gender domination and inequality, with the balance tipped in favour of women not men. On one level this is, of course, very satisfying, but it does mean that gender categories remain largely unquestioned, and it is only with difficulty that gender relations can be reconstituted in the narratives.

Suzy McKee Charnas's novel *Walk to the End of the World* (1974; 1981) bases its account of the relations of power and women's oppression entirely on gender. Charnas has described her book in the following terms:

> It became a story of a society in which power is the crucial question, and the struggle between generations of males is the central form that question takes, while mothers and daughters figure only as labor, brood mares and objects of aggression. The book ended up being about sexism carried to a logical extreme, and it suggests, I hope, the inherent destructiveness of any society in which one portion of the population enslaves and dehumanizes another.[1]

Charnas says of the sequel to the novel, *Motherlines* (1978; 1980), that it

> turned out to be about separatism as a solution to sexism – the heart of the book is the all-woman culture of the 'Riding Women'. Some readers will call the Riding Women monsters, since many people find monstrous the idea of women living good, full lives without men. I do not, though separatism is not my blueprint for Paradise and not the only answer to sexism that I hope to explore in fiction'.[2]

Motherlines is an account of the liberation of women and it is similarly based on what appears to be an unquestioned acceptance of the categories of male and female. In both narratives, differences between women that are determined by race or class, for instance, are subsumed into the universal category of woman. Despite the positive delineation of women-only communities, the narratives are forced to reproduce those patriarchal ways of thinking that they set out to critique because they rely on non-problematised notions of gender.

The context in which the books were written partially explains this dilemma, since the agenda for the feminist movement of the 1970s was set by gender rather than class or race. As Charnas explains:

> Looking back, I now recognize the obvious. During that same winter of 1972–3, I was doing what so many other women were doing and are still doing: reading books like Shulamith Firestone's *The Dialectic*

of Sex (Bantam, 1971) and *Sisterhood is Powerful* edited by Robin Morgan (Vintage, 1970) and participating in consciousness-raising sessions with other women.[3]

By presenting the problem of social change in terms of gender, novels like these were attempting to redefine the dominant ideology. But the separation of gender from other forms of institutionalised oppression means that the narratives reproduce the very ideology to which they are opposed. As Rita Felski suggests:

> The self-recognition of women as an oppressed group is an emancipatory step which makes possible the recognition of and struggle against sexism, but this step is often attained by a suspension of other forms of difference, an erasure felt most painfully by those whose unequal status and particular needs are suppressed by the fiction of a unifying identity.[4]

The prologue to *Walk* provides a fleeting acknowledgement of this problem, but the narrative account of the domination of men over the few remaining resources in a wasted world avoids the question of difference, and refers only to woman as a universal other, seen in the cultural memory of patriarchy as an ever-present threat:

> They remember the evil races whose red skins, brown skins, yellow skins, black skins, skins all the colors of fresh-turned earth marked them as mere treacherous imitations of men, who are white; youths who repudiated their fathers' ways; animals that raided men's crops and waylaid and killed men in the wild places of the world; and most of all the men's own cunning, greedy females. Those were the rebels who caused the downfall of men's righteous rule: men call them 'unmen'. Of all the unmen, only females and their young remain, still the enemies of men.[5]

This litany of patriarchal oppression institutionalises women as the marginalised and dehumanised other in the text. The spacial environment for the oppression of women is the city of Holdfast, where all women are slaves and are considered to be less than human by the men, who both fear and despise them. Love between men is also presented in negative terms in this context, because it is contaminated by the relations of domination that exist in the city. It is the plains and wildernesses far away from the city that provide the environment in which the women who have escaped from the city can live liberated and separate lives, where reproduction itself is possible without men.

Motherlines focuses on two different communities of women, the Free Fems and the Riding Women, and although there are tensions both within and between the communities, they are nevertheless depicted as utopian alternatives. At the end of *Motherlines* there is some suggestion in the narrative that the Free Fems would return to Holdfast to free any remaining fems there. Sarah Lefanu has argued strongly that the books are not essentialist:

> Although there are no male characters in *Motherlines*, Charnas's vision is not an essentialist one. Her Riding Women are strong because they live in freedom, co-operative because coercion has never been forced on them, life-affirming because they know that death is part of life. The question of what women and men are 'naturally' like does not arise; for once, in literature, women have been set free from societal constraints.[6]

This very positive assessment does not quite confront the way in which the narratives fail to escape from the confines of a set of gender assumptions which reproduce the dominant ideology of gender. The women-only communities established in *Motherlines* suggest that women can be free only in the absence of men, a proposition that ironically leaves existing gender relations intact and posits an unproblematic relation between women and the category of Woman.

Charnas's own comment on the books that 'separatism is not my blueprint for Paradise and not the only answer to sexism that I hope to explore in fiction' is an indication of the need for narratives which can go beyond the limits imposed by adherence to a gender classification that is binary in nature. The fact that her next book, *The Vampire Tapestry*, was a novel about a male vampire suggests a recognition that exploration and criticism of gender relations needs a wider frame of reference. Charnas had originally intended to write a book to complete the trilogy, in which the Free Fems would confront and presumably triumph over the misogynist society of Holdfast. However, she later made it clear why the third novel in the trilogy was never written.

> Considering the way things are likely to go in the next decade or so, specifically with regard to the hard-won and now imperiled gains of women and non-whites in America, I don't think anybody who was not insane could actually write that book [*Holdfast Harrowing*]. Someday, maybe, I hope.[7]

A similar problem occurs in another science fiction text from the 1970s written from a feminist perspective, *The Wanderground* (1979; 1985) by Sally Miller Gearhart. In this novel the site of increasingly brutal male domination over women is, once again, the City. To be free from such repression, women have to escape from the cities, and once outside, they can develop an all-women community which exists in complete and mystical harmony with nature. Men are, in effect, confined to the City, because, once outside the City walls, they and their technology are rendered impotent. The powerful and utopian vision of a separate women's community that is offered by the narrative reinforces the exclusivity of the catagories of male and female, even to the extent that the male is associated with technology and the female with life-sustaining qualities. This essentialist view of gender is hardly modified by the presence of the Gentles, those men in the City who are opposed to the violent repression of women and who help the hill women maintain a clandestine observation network in the City:

> About most men here she could give a quick easy answer. About the gentles she could not; her absolutes began to get fuzzy around the edges when she tried to make them apply to a man like Aaron. Even beneath his cultivated hard exterior she could feel his understanding of the essential fundamental knowledge: women and men cannot yet, may not ever, love one another without violence; they are no longer of the same species.[8]

The narrative structure of *The Wanderground* is non-linear and, in science fiction terms, unconventional. The subtitle is *Stories of the hill women* and it consists of interwoven chapters devoted to the individual stories of particular women rather than the development of a storyline which revolves around a central figure. Although this narrative strategy emphasises the collective nature of the women's community, it also by-passes the need to address the problem of gender relations by remaining within an essentialist model in which the binary divsions between nature and culture, male and female are reproduced. The contradictions inherent in these texts stem in part from the attempt to emphasise the utopian possibilites of women-only communities while at the same time resisting the homogenising tendencies of those utopias. In *Motherlines*, there are significant differences and tensions between the groups of women and similarly, the women in *The Wanderground* express deep divisions in their view of the City and the men within it. The most problematic aspect of the women-only communities is that they are depicted as patriarchy's other: they exist by virtue of their opposition to patriarchy and, in the end, all differences are subsumed within that opposition. Patriarchy itself tends to be presented as a homogeneous and unified set of structures which is somehow separate from the subjects who live in it. Although the narratives describe an environment in which women appear to gain access to power and selfhood, they do so in a context in which the very structures which deny women such possibilites remain intact.

This is a dilemma which the narratives are unable to resolve, primarily because they rely on fixed definitions of gender, but also because the notion that subjects interact with the structures in which they find themselves is one that is not explored. This is why Alldera's struggle to become a gendered subject takes place largely at a distance from the brutally repressive structures of Holdfast, and is not shown as having any impact on those structures. At the end of *Walk to the End of the World* it is implied that those structures are collapsing because of their own internal weaknesses. It is difficult to see how a third novel could have been written which both maintained the separatist existence of the women's communities and allowed some re-involvement with Holdfast. Similarly, in *The Wanderground*, there is the unresolved question of the 'gentles', those men who wish to change the structures precisely because they have been influenced by the women. It is arguable that the utopian optimism of the separatist communities depicted in the novels is, in the end, insufficient to sustain a radical critique of patriarchy.

Although James Tiptree Jr's short story 'Houston, Houston, do you read?' (1976; 1978) is also set in a post-holocaust, women-only future, the major concern of the story is with the social and sexual attitudes engendered by patriarchy, rather than the nature of this particular future. The story concerns the three-man crew of an American space craft which is accidently sent three hundred years into the future by solar flare activity. They are rescued by another craft with an all-female crew, and Tiptree uses the central enigma of the unknown nature of this future Earth ironically in the narrative, to reveal the way in which the expectations of both the reader and the spacemen are determined by patriarchal ways of thinking. The men are told that, shortly after their expedition was presumed lost in space, an epidemic ravaged the earth and left the survivors genetically damaged so that no more males could be born. The women themselves are all cloned, which means that in this future the rescued men have no biological function and no power. Only one of the three astronauts can come to terms with this, and he is the one who throughout the narrative has been shown as having the most doubts about his own masculinity.

Tiptree suggests that the reactions of the men depend on the extent to which they are fixed within the determinants of their masculinity. Thus one of them tries to rape a woman and engages in pornographic fantasies about being ruler over all women. Another invokes the patriarchal God of the Old Testament as his rationale for attempting to impose his control and authority over the women, because 'women are not capable of running anything'[9]. Although the narrative is told from the point of view of the three astronauts, their inablility to understand or accept this future is used to undermine their narrative 'authority'. This enables the narrative to question the connection between power and patriarchy. Much of the pleasure in reading this story comes from the way in which the social and sexual hierarchies governing the attitudes and behaviour of the men are satirised by the use of the narrative device of a women-only future in which those hierarchies no longer make sense. By suggesting that masculinity, and the social and sexual relations within which it had meaning, have become anachronisms, Tiptree is able in this short story to focus on the way in which gender relations are constructed.

Tiptree's story marks a change of emphasis in feminist science fiction which can be clearly seen in the next two novels that are discussed, Sheri Tepper's *The Gate to Women's Country* (1988; 1989) and Pamela Sargent's *The Shore of Women* (1986; 1987). In these novels, there is a move away from a definition of the female as patriarchy's other and towards the articulation of a more complex and ambiguous set of gender relations in which representations of masculinity are perceived to be in some sort of crisis. The change of emphasis can be related to the way in which the social and political gains of the 1970s which generated the novels discussed so far were undermined by the political and ideological retrenchment of the 1980s. The restructuring of women's social and political roles that took place as a result of the debates and activities of the 1970s raised profoundly important questions about gender and power. However, the increasing fragmentation of the public sphere in the 1980s has resulted in the significant erosion of the cultural space within which many of the debates were played out.

Enclosure as Feminised Space:
Sheri Tepper's *The Gate to Women's Country* and
Pamela Sargent's *The Shore of Women*

The two novels discussed in this section were written in the 1980s, at a time when questions of social and cultural identity were taking on other dimensions that included, but were different to, gender. *The Shore of Women* and *The Gate to Women's Country* both share a concern with the contradictory and unequal relations within which women and men are positioned as subjects. It is those relations which make the construction of female identity such a complex process of negotiation within structures and between subjects. Although Rita Felski makes no more than a brief reference to the increasing extent of feminist intervention into popular fiction, feminist SF is part of the process described in her discussion of other feminist fictions: 'feminist literature does not reveal an already given female identity, but is itself involved in the construction of this self as a cultural reality'.[10] This account of female identity implies an interaction of the self and the community, which allows for the possibility of dissent, of challenge to sameness, and of the exploration of what such a heterogeneous environment might be like for the female subject.

In looking at female identity from the point of view of its positioning within gender relations, both the novels under discussion are aware of having a certain complicity with the patriarchal structures and attitudes that they wish to criticise. As such they are characterised by that 'doubled vision' described by de Lauretis which results from the consciousness of being both inside and, at the same time, outside the ideology of gender. As a result, the narratives seem less overtly oppositional than the novels of the 1970s, in that they focus more on scrutinising the range of dilemmas and contradictions facing the female subject, rather than eliminating them: they are presented as the raw material out of which the gendered self will emerge. These particular narratives are strikingly similar in that both present post-holocaust, women-only societies in which new definitions of female identity are explored. In these societies, the burden of otherness has shifted from women to men. The narratives explain that men are excluded from positions of power as a consequence of their direct responsibilty for the cataclysm, and to underline the point they are kept physically separate from the women's communities.

From a feminist point of view, novels which describe women-only communities should be considered as utopias, but neither of the narratives in question could be described as being either fully utopian or fully dystopian. They depict societies and subjects which are in a state of flux and uncertainty, and although women are in positions of authority and control over men, anxieties about definitions of both masculinity and femininity are expressed in the narratives. The 'doubled vision' described by de Lauretis is perhaps inevitable given the constraints of the genre, but in these novels it has become an explicit part of the narrative. In this sense they are both complicitous with the ideology of gender as well as opposed to it. Like other postmodern narratives, they never escape what Linda Hutcheon describes as their 'double encoding', by means of which they are 'always aware of the mutual interdependence of the dominant and the contestatory'.[11] They confront the structures of patriarchy which restrict and exclude women and then subvert those structures, firstly by reversing the process to exclude men, and then by questioning the validity of such exclusions. The narratives appropriate the generic convention precisely in order to raise questions about gender relations which cannot otherwise be asked from within the genre.

The issue of whether or not they can be described as utopian or dystopian narratives can be usefully addressed at this point, since the appropriation of the genre also involves the rewriting of assumptions about both utopia and dystopia. Francis Bartkowski suggests that utopias are a means of voicing women's desires, whereas dystopias are a means of suppressing them. She suggests that the utopian novel 'offers a model of how history and the future might be shaped if women were the subjects, that is, speakers of these histories', and she goes on to say that dystopian fictions 'represent the deformation of possible histories and futures when women are silenced'.[12] The expression of female desire is a central feature of feminist science fiction, but so also is the recognition that that desire is marked by its own historical suppression. The clear-cut distinction between utopia and dystopia suggested by Bartkowski does little to explain the way in which feminist science fiction both contests the dominant ideology to celebrate female agency but also recognises the profound limitations on that agency. This is the 'doubled vision' that makes it difficult to label the narratives either utopian or dystopian – they are essentially a mixture of the two modes.

The issue is characterised slightly differently by Søren Baggeson, who describes science fiction as 'basically a utopian mode of story-telling' which changed to a 'dystopian mode' characterised by a prevailing pessimism.[13] Instead of referring to utopia and dystopia as distinct tropes, he chooses to describe them in terms of 'utopian pessimism' or 'dystopian pessimism'. Both are considered to be oppositional forms but the latter closes down around the possibilities for change, whereas the former keeps intact its capacity to intervene in material conditions and remake them in some way. These kinds of texts are, therefore, open-ended. Although Baggeson's analysis remains at the level of abstraction because it takes no account of gender, his use of the thoroughly contradictory term 'utopian pessimism' is nevertheless an interesting one, because it recognises the complex nature of particular kinds of science fiction texts.

That complexity is also recognised in Tom Moylan's study of science fiction, in which he makes a distinction between what he calls the 'literary utopia' and the 'critical utopia'. For Moylan, 'utopia' has been appropriated by hegemonic structures as part of the process by which the dominant ideology and structures are maintained. In particular, consumer society has co-opted utopian longing to itself in order to render us passive. Moylan locates the revival of the subversive intent of utopia within the emergence of the 'critical utopia' from the oppositional culture of the 1960s and 1970s:

> Inspired by the movements of the 1960s and finding new imagery in the alternatives being explored in the 1970s, the critical utopia is part of the political practice and visions shared by a variety of autonomous oppositional movements that reject the domination of the emerging system of transnational corporations and post-industrial production and ideological structures.[14]

For Moylan, the 'critical utopia' 'creates a neutral space in which opposition can be articulated and received'.[15] Moylan's account does not fully recognise the importance of difference, and his use of the term 'critical utopia' suggests that all oppositional groups will share the same understanding of what 'utopia' is, by virtue of being oppositional. He also underestimates the impact of gender ideology by suggesting that there can be such a thing as a gender-free 'neutral space'. Even so, the use of the term 'critical utopia' does help towards an understanding of the way in which feminist science fiction seeks to interrogate existing gender relations.

Constance Penley, on the other hand, uses the term 'critical dystopia' to take issue with Fredric Jameson's claim that science fiction's fantasies of the future demonstrate the atrophy of the utopian imagination which has resulted in 'our incapacity to imagine the future'. According to Jameson, the role of science fiction is to reveal to us our own cultural and ideological limits by showing us the present represented as history, which is why science fiction seems so preoccupied with dystopia. Penley prefers the term 'critical dystopia', arguing that some dystopias are capable of adopting a more critical perspective towards the present than others. Thus, a film like *The Terminator* is a critical dystopia because 'it tends to suggest causes rather than merely reveal symptoms',[16] and by transferring the perceived consequences of the social and cultural trends of the present to the future, those trends can be obliquely criticised. What all of these views suggest is that contemporary science fiction texts increasingly include both utopian and dystopian elements, and that what they have in common is the way in which they critically voice the fears and anxieties of a range of new and fragmented social and sexual constituencies and identities in post-industrial societies.

The inclusion of both utopian and dystopian characteristics within the same text is a feature of both feminist and postmodern writing, in which the totalising tendencies of the dominant ideology are challenged from a variety of different perspectives. The novels under discussion in this section are part of the struggle to articulate the emergence of the female subject in a context in which female agency continues to experience profound limitations. The post-modern uncertainty generated in the narratives derives from the disruption of genre expectations and also from the perspective the narratives provide on contemporary social and sexual relations. As in all disaster narratives, the dominant anxieties of the present are projected into a future suffering the effects of a major calamity. The past in which that calamity took place is, in effect, our own present, and a critique of the repressions and inequalities of the present can therefore be offered from the vantage point of the fictional future of these narratives.

Post-holocaust novels written from a non-feminist point of view often show the gender ideology of the present being re-established unquestioningly in the future, so that Oedipal narratives survive intact whatever the nature of the disaster. However, the 'speculative fiction of survival by women' described by Maria Minich Brewer allows women writers to

> rewrite the Oedipal conflict into their texts by assigning it a limited place and a place limited historically (in the past and present). That is, they situate it with respect to their global conception of a different narrative of gender (in the future).[17]

Thus, in *The Gate to Women's Country*, the Oedipal narrative of conflict which resulted in the cataclysm is relegated to history:

> Three hundred years ago almost everyone in the world had died in a great devastation brought about by men. It was men who made the weapons and men who were the diplomats and men who made the speeches about national pride and defense. And in the end it was men who did whatever they had to do, pushed the buttons or pulled the string to set the terrible things off.[18]

In the novel, Tepper describes a society in which the legacy of the 'convulsions' is that new sets of social and sexual relations have been established within which women dominate, and in which the version of masculinity which depends on aggression and hierarchy is marginalised.

After the cataclysm, each new town that was established had a defensive garrison attached to it, outside the city walls, but controlled by the women. This is where the majority of men remain and garrison life is used as a metaphor for what has become a ritualised version of masculinity. The men from the garrisons and the women from Women's Country meet socially and sexually only at carnival time. At the age of five, male children are handed over to the garrison by their mothers, after which they return home to Women's Country only for holidays, and are given the final choice of remaining with the garrison or returning to Women's Country when they are fifteen. This acts as a weeding-out process to ensure that those who do return are fully committed to relinquishing the masculinist values of the garrison and can accept their status as 'servitors' in Women's Country. What this means in practice is that Women's Country is governed by women, but that the servitors are party to decisions made by the women, and help carry out those decisions. In other words, they have considerable autonomy, and the narrative hints at the utopian possibility of genuine equality in the future.

Almost as if to undermine that possibility, however, there is a considerable emphasis in the narrative on enclosure and uncertainty. Walls and boundaries dominate the narrative: the cities are walled and access to them is gained only through the ritually named 'Gate to Women's Country'. These boundaries are metaphors for sexual and psychic difference, and the physical separation of the men who live as 'warriors' in the garrisons from the women who control Women's Country is emblematic of the novel's concern with gender relations. Walls and gates signify those ideologically created boundaries between gendered subjects which it is the project of the novel to question. One way in which this is done is through the distinction that is made in the narrative between different kinds of masculinity. The masculinity of the garrison 'warriors' is encoded in hierarchies, rituals and routines which emphasise glory, honour and war:

> The feet of the men falling in unison, the whip and snap of the banners, the ribbons, the plumes, and the drums, the drums. Honour, the trumpets cried. Honour, the drums beat home. Power, the garrison cried. (132)

The men who choose to leave the garrisons to return to Women's Country are described by the remaining warriors as 'titsuckers' or 'weirds'. In fact, theirs is a differently defined masculinity, not only because they have chosen to return to Women's Country, but also because increasing numbers of them have developed psychic abilities. These abilities enable them to 'see' in a psychic sense but also to 'see through' the self-deceptive masculine ideology of those who remain in the garrisons. Although the narrative suggests that this is not an absolutely gender-specific ability, its function is clearly to indicate that men need it more than women.

One of the secrets of Women's Country is that it is the servitors who father most of the children, and it is hoped that increasing numbers of male children will inherit psychic abilities and choose to return to Women's Country. This piece of social engineering is entirely unknown to the warriors, so that their perception of themselves as indispensable to all women, and of the servitors as men who are 'gelded' on their return to Women's Country, is treated very ironically in the narrative. The nature of the boundaries between gendered subjects is also questioned by means of the central female character, Stavia, whose unsuccessful relationship with the warrior Chernon is used to explore the contradictions of social and sexual relations which are determined by gender ideology. She is motivated both by sexual desire and also by what she believes is love for the warrior, but she underestimates the extent to which he is bound by his own masculinity. His interest in her is motivated by conflicting desires, the desire for a son of his 'own', the desire to know what he describes as the 'secrets' of the women, all of which take little account of her sense of herself as an autonomous subject. Although she has a son as a result of her relationship with Chernon, the boy decides to remain with the garrison when he is old enough to choose. The relationship symbolises the polarities on which the narrative is built: Women's Country enables Stavia to develop knowledge of herself as a female subject but this is undermined by the patriarchal social relations which determine Chernon's attitudes. Stavia ultimately finds a fulfilling relationship with Corrig, a servitor, rather than a warrior. It is the unresolved conflict between different definitions of masculinity which undermines the potentially utopian aspects of Women's Country.

A further textual device used to explore this idea is that of the play performed ritually every year in Women's Country, *Iphegenia at Ilium*, which is an ironic retelling of the story of the fall of Troy, from the point of view of the women who were the silenced victims. It runs in counterpoint to the myth of Telemachus and Odysseus, which is used by the garrisons to symbolise their sense of the power of their own masculinity. The women's play parodies the heroic actions of the warriors at the seige of Troy, by suggesting that the way in which aggression is represented as heroism is part of the ideological work of patriarchy. The final lines of the play are spoken to Achilles and they act as a statement about the position of women under patriarchy:

> HECUBA . . . Dead or damned, that's the choice we make. Either you men kill us and are honoured for it, or we women kill you and are damned for it. Dead or damned. Women don't have to make choices like that in Hades. There's no love there, nothing to betray.
> ACHILLES (*Shaking his head, still weeping*) I ask you yet again, Agamemnon's daughter. What's it like, this Hades!
> IPHIGENIA What's Hades like?
> Like dream without waking. Like carrying water in a sieve. Like coming into harbor after storm. Barren harbor where the empty river runs through an endless desert into the sea. Where all the burdens have been taken away.
> You'll understand when you come there at last, Achilles. . . .
> Hades is Women's Country. (278)

This description of Women's Country as Hades is double-edged. It expresses the gulf between the new gender relations of Women's Country and the patriarchal relations of the garrisons, and it is also a narrative reference to the way in which the women deal with the aggressive masculinity of the garrisons. Because the warriors are convinced of their own superiority and autonomy, they are periodically driven to attempt to take power from the women. The women in the different towns, together with the servitors, deal with such conspiracies by organising wars between the garrisons which ensure that the conspirators are wiped out and the towns remain safe from the threat of male aggresson. More particularly, the image of Hades also draws attention to the gendered position of the narrative within the genre of science fiction. Its project has been to enable female subjectivity to become a legitimate focus of the science fiction narrative without having to propose essentialist definitions of gender. The narrative attempts to be both an avowal of feminism and a statement of the need for masculinity to confront its own myths.

However, the dominant textual metaphors of boundaries and walls indicate unresolved textual ambiguities regarding the reconceptualising of gender. The narrative suggests that the city provides a new space in which the female self is no longer contained by masculine assumptions about gender. But at the same time, the secure walls of the city behind which the women shelter continue to invoke ideas of limitation, of struggle to remain in control in the hostile environment created by masculine assumptions about gender, and denial of female instrumentality. The place that is Women's Country represents the utopian and dystopian possibilities of a contemporary social and cultural environment in which the disintegration of familiar social structures and networks can lead to the formation of new demands, and new relations. *The Gate to Women's Country* moves away from earlier depictions of women-only communities by focusing on the instability of social relations and the risks involved in the formation of new subjects and subject relations.

A similar set of concerns is articulated in Pamela Sargent's *The Shore of Women*. This story is also set in a future in which the earth has been devastated by the uncontrolled and aggressive use of technology. During the centuries of recovery after what is described as the 'Destruction', power has shifted to the female survivors. They build walled and technologically sophisticated cities from which men are excluded altogether. In this future, there is an absolute gender division which is both physical and cultural, the rationale for which is the inherently aggressive nature of the male, which precipitated the Destruction. Men are effectively banished to the wilderness outside the cities to survive in stone-age conditions as best they can. In the feminist narratives of the 1970s, women found their freedom away from the cities, in the wilderness. Both Sargent and Tepper redefine the relationships between nature, culture and gender so that the city becomes the site of female empowerment, while the outside or the wilderness symbolises the disempowerment of the masculine.

In Sargent's novel, men are denied access to any kind of technology, and they are not permitted to establish any form of social organisation more complex than a tribal structure. Those men who attempt to do so are killed by the destructive weapons of the cities. A form of religion based on the 'Lady', the earth goddess, loosely prevails in the cities, but it is imposed on men in order to provide a cultural rationale that is part myth, part history, for their absolute exclusion from the cities. Shrines in which men can worship 'the Lady' have been erected in the wilderness and as well as being used to instil superstitious fear of the Lady into the men, the shrines also function as electronically controlled listening posts for the city women. By means of the shrines, men are periodically summoned to the city walls in order to become sperm donors for the women's programme of artificial insemination, since physical contact with men is regarded as abhorrent by the women.

The quasi-religious doctrine of the Lady has a double function in the narrative: since it emerged after the cataclysm, it implies a critique of contemporary patriarchal structures, but, more significantly, it is used to establish an ironic and critical distance from the ritualised aspects of this women-only society:

> Once, women had given men the power over life that women had held since the beginning of human history; so we have all been taught. Men had used their power for evil, and the world had been devastated and poisoned in ancient times by the weapons men had controlled. The great fire came and, after it, the long winter.[19]

Long after this came the 'Rebirth', when cities were rebuilt in areas away from the greatest devastation. In the women's doctrine, this signalled the point in their history when the 'ten thousand years of man's rule, an aberration in human history, were past' (97). Women are taught that the exclusion of men from the cities is essential to ensure the survival of humankind:

> men had a propensity for violence that was both genetic and hormonal. The biological wellbeing of humankind as a whole required some of their qualities, but the survival of civilization demanded that women, who were less driven and able to channel their aggressiveness constructively, remain in control. (92)

That the text is not going to endorse the essentialist view of gender put forward in this conflation of history and religious doctrine is made clear by the flat and virtually toneless language in which it is recounted, as well as by the fact that Laissa, who is the speaker, is beginning to question the received doctrine. This lack of endorsement produces a certain textual equivocation towards the critique of contemporary patriarchy that is implied in the narrative. The question of where to locate that critique haunts the narrative and partially explains why the novel focuses so intently on the development of identity within reconfigured relationships which are at odds with the prevailing values of the cities. The cities within which all women live have suppressed their utopian possibilities and are described as having become intellectually and socially moribund, so that few question the structures under which they live. There is an oblique suggestion that the cities reproduce many of the repressive aspects of patriarchy, particularly the way in which social and cultural absolutes are built on gender differences. Even within the cities, difference is perceived as threat, for which the most extreme form of punishment is exile from the city.

The narrative is divided into three voices and what they have in common is the fact that each of the three characters is marginalised in some way from the dominant structures. Each is engaged in a struggle to achieve a gendered selfhood in opposition to those structures. One voice belongs to Birana, a young woman whose mother commits the crime of wounding another woman: for that she is punished by exile from the city, and Birana with her. Exile is the equivalent of a death sentence, since women do not know how to survive in the wilderness, nor are they intended to. The second voice is that of Laissa, a one-time friend of Birana, who is destined to become one of the 'Mothers of the City', the educated power elite which takes responsibility both for government and for bearing male children. In a similar device to that used in *The Gate to Women's Country*, male children are given to their genetic fathers in the wilderness when they are five years old. The third voice is that of Arvil, Laissa's twin brother, who was taken outside the walls to his genetic father years earlier.

The narrative explores the process by which each of the characters is required to transgress the physical and cultural boundaries shaping their perceptions, in order to change and progress. Although Birana's mother is killed in the wilderness, ironically enough because her clothing made her look like a man, Birana survives long enough to be rescued by Arvil from the shrine where she had taken shelter. The narrative follows the progress of Birana and Arvil as they move into the wilderness to conceal Birana's survival from the women in the city. Their journey is both real and symbolic, and is used as the means to explore the way in which gender ideology informs all human activity. Arvil has to overcome his deeply ingrained fear of Birana's femaleness before he can stop seeing her as an earthly embodiment of the Goddess, who is the source of both fear and pleasure. Birana has to have Arvil's protection in the wilderness in order to survive, but she sees all men as animals until she has acquired enough understanding to begin to see qualities and differences amongst them.

In what seems to be an allusion to *Walk to the End of the World*, a quest element is introduced into the narrative: Birana believes that there is a colony of exiled women who have survived in the wilderness and enlists Arvil's aid to find it. Since it is never found, however, the real journey is clearly one of self-discovery for both Birana and Arvil, to find a selfhood outside the confines of gender ideology which can encompass sexual desire within a reconfigured set of gender relations. Laissa, too, moves from being a character who subscribes absolutely to the structures and rules of the city to being one who can perceive the need for those structures to change. She begins to question the version of the past offered in the doctrines taught in the city: 'The more we learn about the outside, the more we'll be able to distinguish a true danger from something we can leave alone. We've been hiding in our cities too long' (438). She breaks the city's rules by listening to and recording the story of Birana and Arvil, and is entrusted by them with their child, which, since it is female, will be alowed to remain within the city rather than endure life in the wilderness. Laissa is punished for her relationship with the exiled Birana by a kind of internal exile within the city, whereby she is denied her role as a 'Mother' of the city. Despite this, she has been empowered by her transgression and becomes capable of asking the kinds of critical questions about existing structures and relations that have been suppressed.

What is striking about the narrative is that, although the three characters move towards a different sense of self, none of them achieve any kind of social integration. Birana and Arvil remain in the wilderness where their chances of survival are slim, and Laissa remains a marginalised figure within the city. This inevitably draws attention to the equivocal position of the text as feminist science fiction; although female desire can be foregrounded in such marginalised texts, it is also contained within gender ideology, which determines definitions of self and maintains the boundaries between self and community. Such texts have constantly to negotiate their relationship to that ideology and this can result in conflicting and contradictory representations of both gender and desire. Female desire is explored in the text both through the relationships between women in the city and through the relationship that develops between Birana and Arvil. Despite this attempt at representational even-handedness, the dominant frame of reference of the narrative is defined by heterosexuality, as is made clear by the nostalgic overtones of romance fiction in the final paragraph of the novel:

> There is no word of Birana's fate or of Arvil's, no sign that they live, no rumour that they have been seen outside. Yet I cannot think of them as dead. They live on in my mind, freed by their love from her world and his. I imagine them on a distant shore near a refuge they have built for themselves dreaming of the oceans we might sail again and the stars we might seek. Perhaps we will join them on that shore at last. (469)

Looked at slightly differently, however, these lines enable us to focus on the limits of gender ideology. The relationship between Birana and Arvil remains an isolated event which has little immediate impact on the city or its values. The reconciliation of the emerging female subject with the masculinity of a 'new man' like Arvil is not achieved in the text, although it is made clear at the end of the novel that such a reconciliation is desirable. The central problem of how to incorporate masculinity into the potentially utopian aspects of the female community of the city proves impossible to resolve in the text, and the contradictory and incomplete definitions of both desire and identity remain sharply in focus. Laissa's account of the relationship between Birana and Arvil concludes with an overt statement of the need for change:

> We were forced to choose this pattern once because our survival was at stake. I believe it may be at stake once more. We may stagnate, as life does when it holds to a pattern that is no longer needed, which can keep it from growing and becoming something more. It may be time for us and for those outside to begin to reshape ourselves and become another kind of being. (468–9)

Although there is a certain triteness to this statement which is echoed elsewhere in the language of the novel, it is also an indication of the way in which the narrative is attempting to move into a debate which allows for the fact that it is struggling with the politics of diversity, where the issue has become more than one of inclusion or exclusion, and where identity is always in the process of becoming. The walls behind which the women of these future societies shelter have a double meaning: they both contain but at the same time they create a space within which the gendered subject can develop. However, it also has to be remembered that the women in these narratives remain within walls that have been erected in the future because of the patriarchal attitudes of the present. Demands for the recognition of the authenticity of the female subject remain incompatible with patriarchy, and so in these narratives the female communities remain enclosed and contained. By feminising these spaces, the narratives atempt to overcome the negative connotations of such enclosure.

Margaret Atwood: *The Handmaid's Tale* as a Critical Dystopia

Enclosure is depicted in unequivocally negative terms in Margaret Atwood's ironic near-future dystopia, *The Handmaid's Tale* (1986; 1987). The narrative depicts the social and psychic confinement that women are subjected to in the Republic of Gilead, which is intended to supress female agency altogether by erasing the presence of women from the arena of public life. Gilead came into being after a conservative coup known as the 'President's Day massacre' installed a new christian fundamentalist regime in what was formerly the

United States. It is a state in which inequality has been elevated to become a founding political principle, and as such it is the embodiment of patriarchal beliefs about gender. The impact of the narrative stems from the fact that its critique of patriarchy is set in the more general context of a critique of contemporary gender politics: Atwood examines the way in which the hegemonic structures of patriarchy both repress women and invite them to collude in their own repression. She uses the familiar metaphor of the totalitarian state to represent patriarchal hegemony, which is seen through the eyes of an almost anonymous narrator, whose most outstanding characteristic appears to be her passivity. The narrative suggests that this passivity is only partly the result of the brutal 're-education' process she has undergone in the new regime, and that in a generalised fashion it may have been a contributory factor in the rise of extreme fundamentalism.

The narrator's memories of her life in pre-Gilead times are juxtaposed against her present restricted existence and through this device the narrative suggests that most of the features of the masculine hegemony were already in place. The main difference between 'then' and 'now' is that this hegemony has become overtly repressive. She remembers how she felt immediately after she has lost her job, like every other woman in the newly proclaimed state:

> What's the matter? he said.
> I don't know, I said.
> We still have . . . he said. But he didn't go on to say what we still had. It occurred to me that he shouldn't be saying *we*, since nothing that I knew of had been taken away from him.
> We still have each other, I said. It was true. Then why did I sound, even to myself, so indifferent?
> He kissed me then, as if now I'd said that, things could get back to normal. But something had shifted, some balance. I felt shrunken, so that when he put his arms around me, gathering me up, I was small as a doll. I felt love going forward without me.
> He doesn't mind this, I thought. He doesn't mind it at all. Maybe he even likes it. We are not each other's any more. Instead, I am his.[20]

Atwood's ironic exaggeration of patriarchy draws specific attention to the social and sexual positioning of women, but also to the difficulties of articulating an oppositional response to that positioning which does not become essentialist or separatist.

This extrapolation of gender attitudes from the present into the

near future underlines the growing influence of the rhetoric of the
conservative moral majority throughout the 1980s, as well as the
systematic erosion of many of the rights for women that were gained
in the 1960s and 1970s. Gilead provides Atwood with a framework
for exploring the considerable success with which the New Right has
sought to establish control of the moral high ground, despite the
increasing challenges to existing patriarchal and hierarchical forms
of political and cultural authority. Anxieties about changes in
contemporary social and cultural structures are very often expressed
through demands for the restoration of an idealised past in which
family, state and nation are seen as virtually synonymous. Atwood
has taken this rhetoric literally in order to create the nightmare state
of Gilead, rather than examining the actual social and political
reality behind the rhetoric. She comments on this in an interview:

> There are lots of people who say, 'Women's place is in the home', and
> who think, 'Oh yes, that's right.' But people do not think it through.
> They don't think in the concrete, day-to-day, what-will-it-smell-like
> detail. So it's all very well to say, 'Women should be back in the home.'
> That's an abstract statement. It doesn't threaten anybody because it's
> 'women'. It's that thing called 'women' and you can talk about
> 'women' as if the group doesn't include anybody we know.[21]

Atwood's dystopia places women's experience of the repressive
structures of patriarchy as central to the narrative, and it also
extrapolates from the moral panics around the rapidly changing
nature of that experience.

The intention of the new state of Gilead is to restore things to
'Nature's norm', by removing the social and economic gains
painstakingly made by women in the struggle for equal rights.
Women are disempowered in the new regime by the passing of a law
which forbids them to work or to own property, thus depriving them
of their economic independence. Most women are re-assigned to
social roles that accord with patriarchal notions of gender, and so
they become wives, breeders, servants or prostitutes. Whatever
status they have is acquired through marriage, because they can bear
children, or because they are ideologically committed to the new
state. Only the 'Unwomen' have no status. These are the women who
cannot or will not fit into the new structures, and who are sent to
the 'colonies' as labourers or to state brothels. In either case, they
are rendered invisible in the fabric of Gileadean society.

Hierarchical structures, ritualised behaviour and codes of dress are used to reinforce gender identity at the expense of personal identity, and in an ironic re-use of contemporary cultural attitudes, Atwood depicts women's clothing as a sign of repression rather than an expression of self-definition. In this semiotic system handmaids wear red, wives wear patrician blue, domestic workers wear green, and econowives wear red, blue and green striped dresses since they are expected to perform all three functions. The dress of the handmaids is the most explicitly symbolic, as is their social role. It consists of a long red dress and a white head covering with wings that are designed to conceal both their bodies and their identities, from themselves as much as from the world. The confining nature of the dress reproduces the kind of existence that has been imposed on women in the new state:

> Given our wings, our blinkers, it's hard to look up, hard to get the full view, of the sky, of anything. But we can do it, a little at a time, a quick move of the head, up and down, to the side and back. We have learned to see the world in gasps. (40)

The idea of seeing the world in 'gasps' is echoed throughout the narrative, where pieces of the narrator's past are juxtaposed against aspects of the present to conjure up a sense of personal and cultural confusion and displacement.

One of the strengths of Atwood's writing is that it suggests how the familiar and the taken for granted can be transformed with relative ease into structures of oppression. As Atwood herself has insisted, the dystopian near future of Gilead contains nothing new, it is simply given a different emphasis. In a world where pollution and disease have made increasing numbers of men and women infertile, women who can bear children are forced to become breeders or 'handmaids', a title derived from the biblical relationship between the childless Rachel and her maid Bilhah. This enforced surrogate motherhood is legitimised in a bizarre monthly 'ceremony' in which the head of the household, the 'Commander', attempts to impregnate his allocated handmaid while she lies between the legs of his ageing or sterile wife. Handmaids take the names of their current commander, and so the narrator is known only as Offred, which signifies her status as handmaid to Fred, a Commander in the Gilead hierarchy. Her name has been taken from her as part of the process of 're-education', and the details of her previous life have been almost obliterated from her own memory. Like all women in Gilead, she has been constructed in another image drawn from the cultural memories of patriarchy. As Offred says: 'My self is a thing I must now compose, as one composes a speech. What I must present is a made thing, not something born' (76). The narrative emphasises that Offred, like Gilead itself, has been constructed, or rather reconstructed, from materials that already exist. It is only as Offred recalls the past from within the oppressive conditions of the present that she can understand how Gilead already existed as a possibility that was simply not recognised:

> Is that how we lived then? But we lived as usual. Everyone does, most of the time. Whatever is going on is as usual. Even this is as usual, now. We lived, as usual, by ignoring. Ignoring isn't the same as ignorance, you have to work at it. (66)

The remaking of the female subject in patriarchal terms in Gilead is achieved through an appropriation of the rhetoric of feminism, which is then relocated within the discourses of patriarchy to justify the oppression of women. Offred's commander re-uses recognisable elements of feminist critiques of patriarchal society to suggest that women are better off under the new regime because they are so central to its philosophy:

> We've given them more than we've taken away, said the Commander. Think of the trouble they had before. Don't you remember the singles bars, the indignity of high-school blind dates? The meat market. Don't you remember the terrible gap between the ones who could get a man easily and the ones who couldn't? Some of them were desperate, they starved themselves thin or pumped their breasts full of silicone, had their noses cut off. Think of the human misery. . . .
> This way they're protected, they can fulfill their biological destinies in peace. With full support and encouragement. (231)

The hegemonising process is also visible in the way in which the state uses women to police other women: known as the 'Aunts', they are the chief instruments of the brutal re-education imposed on those women who are reluctant to accept their role as handmaids. In a parody of contemporary feminism, the Aunts repeatedly invoke the need for a women's culture and community in the interests of Gilead's fundamentalist patriarchal regime: 'What we're aiming for, says Aunt Lydia, is a spirit of camaraderie among women. We must all pull together' (234).

The narrative suggests that ambivalence towards feminism on the part of women has in part been responsible for the ascendency of the repressive politics of the New Right. Offred's recollections of her relationship with her radical feminist mother make this point. She recalls feeling both embarrassed and oppressed by her mother's commitment to radical feminism, since she herself had no strong feelings about it. This ambivalence provides one of the most ironic moments of the narrative, when, after the obligatory communal participation in the birth of another handmaid's child, Offred comments: 'Mother, I think. Wherever you may be. Can you hear me? You wanted a women's culture. Well, now there is one. It isn't what you meant, but it exists' (137). Offred has, by implication, colluded in the emergence of Gilead through her own indifference, and when one of the Aunts declares that 'Gilead is within you' (33), this emphasises the way in which patriarchal hegemony is maintained not by means of force but through the ideology of gender. Appropriation and redefinition are thus presented as part of the process by which oppositional and often incoherent forces can be usurped in the interests of a conservative hegemony such as that represented by Gilead.

Motifs of construction and reconstruction are used in the narrative to emphasise the unilinear logic of patriarchy. The narrative itself is revealed as a reconstruction in the concluding 'Historical Notes' which contextualise Gilead as merely a moment in history which has become a suitable subject for a historical research conference. The fact that Gilead is sandwiched between a past in which it existed only as a possibility, as seen through Offred's memories, and a future in which its only existence is as a historical curiosity, suggests that the narrative is more concerned with the metaphoric content of Gilead than with any concrete realisation of the nature of the new state. As a result, the narrative can offer a powerful if generalised sense of the contemporary conflict of ideologies which has not yet been resolved. Criticism of Atwood's novel has concentrated on the fact that the details of Gilead are too vague to make her dystopia convincing, as was suggested in Mary McCarthy's somewhat dismissive review of the novel in *The New York Times Book Review*:

> The author has carefully drawn her projections from current trends. As she has said elsewhere, there is nothing here that has not been anticipated in the United States of America that we already know.

Perhaps that is the trouble: the projections are too neatly pencilled in.
The details . . . all raise their hands announcing themselves present.
At the same time, the Republic of Gilead itself, whatever in it that is
not a projection, is insufficiently imagined.[22]

If Gilead appears somewhat provisional, it is because Atwood is not
suggesting that it is an inevitable outcome of 'current trends'. As was
indicated earlier in the discussion, it is a particular kind of rhetoric
from which she has extrapolated to create Gilead, rather than actual
trends. The novel constitutes an intervention into those discourses
of the new right which are organised so powerfully around the
family, heterosexuality and gender identity, and which are constituted in dystopian terms in the imagined state of Gilead.

The dystopian characteristics of the narrative are, however,
strategically undermined by the Historical Notes at the end of the
narrative, which purport to be from the 'Twelfth Symposium on
Gileadean Studies' held in 2195. The perspective provided by the
Notes indicates that Gilead has, in fact, no future, and it does not,
therefore, have history on its side. The archaicism adopted in Gilead
ironically anticipates its own demise. Repeated references throughout the text to images of construction and reconstruction suggest
that the existing ideas and practices that gave rise to the short-lived
state of Gilead are just as available for the imagining of other forms
of social and cultural relations, other kinds of reconstructions. The
Historical Notes inform us that the narrative is reconstructed from
tapes made by Offred, and Offred describes herself as a thing not
born but made. She comments ambiguously at one point in her
account that: 'This is a reconstruction. All of it is a reconstruction'
(144). While this could refer to the retrospective nature of Offred's
account as well as to the fact that Gilead is an attempt to
institutionalise particular forms of patriarchy, its chief function is to
serve as a reminder of the fictionality of the narrative. The self-
reflexivity of the text becomes the means by which Atwood can
challenge the dystopian assumption of inevitability that is seemingly
written into the text. The open-ended narrative leaves the reader in
doubt as to Offred's eventual fate, and the Historical Notes provide
no real indication of the dystopian or utopian nature of the possible
future that they inhabit.

The focus of Atwood's criticism is, then, the gender relations
and politics of patriarchy, and the narrative is concerned to present
Gilead as one possible outcome of those relations and politics, but

not necessarily the only one. While it is not Atwood's intention to articulate a specific political agenda, the novel nevertheless makes an intervention into the moral and ideological territory colonised by the New Right. The use of the future fiction form to make this intervention is interesting because it cuts across publishing, marketing and readership boundaries, and enables Atwood to draw on motifs not usually available to her as a mainstream writer. She employs irony to expose the ideological practices of patriarchy without suggesting that those practices are so powerfully entrenched that they cannot be challenged. As a critical dystopia, *The Handmaid's Tale* is not concerned to portray the inevitability and awfulness of a future in which patriarchy has become fully totalitarian. Instead, the kind of extrapolation used in the novel alerts us to the necessity to rethink the forms which contemporary gender relations take. The metaphor of the narrative as a series of reconstructions indicates the provisionality of those relations, not their permanence.

Chapter 5

Cyberpunk, Cyborgs and Feminist Science Fiction

The Radical Anxieties of Cyberpunk

In many ways the most significant intervention into the science fiction genre in the 1980s has been cyberpunk. Although the term was coined initially to describe William Gibson's first novel *Neuromancer* (1984; 1986), it has acquired such cultural resonance that it has since been applied to a far wider range of cultural products, and unconscious traces of cyberpunk[1] are now seen everywhere, particularly in films such as *Blade Runner* and *Brazil*, and in the work of writers such as William Burroughs and Thomas Pynchon. Cyberpunk writers acknowledge their own literary debt to Burroughs and Pynchon, as well as to New Wave writers from the 1960s and 1970s such as J.G. Ballard and Samuel Delany. What is noticeably absent from the many public declarations or 'manifestos' made by, and on behalf of, cyberpunk writers is any acknowledgement of the equally profound influence of feminist science fiction. This chapter will explore the relationship between cyberpunk and feminist science fiction, and will also attempt to discover what, if anything, cyberpunk has to offer feminist SF.

It is cyberpunk's 'patriarchal nervousness', suggests Samuel Delany, that prevents it from acknowledging feminist science fiction as an 'absent Mother':

> the feminist explosion – which obviously infiltrates the cyberpunk writers so much – is the one they seem to be the least comfortable with, even though it's one that, much more than the New Wave, has influenced them most strongly, both in progressive and in reactionary ways.[2]

It is no surprise that cyberpunk is strongly inscribed with the masculine, since the heroes of cyberpunk are drawn from the high-tech environment of hackers and rock music, and the rhetoric echoes that which is found in the narratives of detective and adventure fiction. However, this does not mean that cyberpunk has nothing to offer feminists or that it has not had an influence of its own on contemporary feminist science fiction. Joan Gordon argues that cyberpunk is a potentially enriching source of ideas for contemporary feminist writers:

> Egalitarian toughness makes the women of male-dominated cyberpunk politically appealing to feminists, but cyberpunk has something more important and less direct to offer as well: a vision of the world which is both a logical extension of the 1980s and a radical departure from the essentially nostalgic view of feminist science fiction.[3]

Although a preoccupation with 'nostalgia' and an apparent unwillingness to tackle 'hard science' is a recognisable aspect of some feminist SF, the interface between human and machine has also been an on-going concern, as previous discussion has indicated. There has been a recognition in feminist science fiction that, as Teresa de Lauretis suggests, technology 'shapes our perception and cognitive processes, mediates our relationships with objects of the material and physical world, and our relationships with our own or other bodies'.[4] Technology, then, provides the context in which both cyberpunk and feminist science fiction deal with the central questions of difference and identity in a post-industrial, postmodern society.

Cyberpunk has been described as the 'apotheosis' of postmodernism by Istvan Csicsery-Ronay, and as its 'truest and most consistent incarnation, bar none'.[5] In his introduction to the cyberpunk edition of *Missippi Review*, Larry McCaffery is of the opinion that 'cyberpunk seems to be the only art systematically dealing with the most crucial political, philosophical, moral, and cultural issues of our day'.[6] Science fiction writer Gregory Benford has characterised it in a less flattering light as simply 'a marketing strategy masquerading as a literary movement'.[7] Central to cyberpunk is its identification with the iconoclastic and counter-cultural ethos of both punk and rock music; it has been defined by cyberpunk writer Bruce Sterling as part of a 'new alliance . . . an integration of technology and the Eighties counterculture'.[8] Cyberpunk's counter-cultural credentials were enhanced by the report of a US Secret Service raid on the offices of a company developing a cyberpunk role-play game, presumably because some of the research for the game focused on hacking.[9] Whilst claims that cyberpunk constitutes a movement of radical and even revolutionary significance are difficult to substantiate, it nevertheless appears to represent science fiction's most vigorous response to the kinds of organisational and technological transformations in production and consumption that are characteristic of post-industrial, postmodern societies.

Cyberpunk narratives focus explicitly on the destabilising impact of new technology on traditional social and cultural spaces: in so doing they provide a peculiarly appropriate response to the complex conditions of postmodernity, particularly the collapse of traditional cultural and critical hierarchies, and the erosion of the distinction between experience and knowledge which has provoked the decentring and fragmentation of the subject. These are also key issues in feminist science fiction, without which, Samuel Delany argues, 'there wouldn't *be* any cyberpunk'. In other words, feminist SF has provided cyberpunk with a conceptual vocabulary, 'without which we wouldn't be able to read it'.[10] The collection of cyberpunk stories edited by Bruce Sterling, *Mirrorshades* (1986; 1988), contains an introduction that is widely regarded as a cyberpunk 'manifesto' in which Sterling, as spokesman for 'The Movement', describes cyberpunks as a group whose 'precursors are legion' and which is 'steeped in the lore and tradition of the SF field'. It is noticeable, however, that none of the precursors named by Sterling is a woman; the impact of feminist science fiction writers on the genre goes equally unacknowledged in Sterling's preface to *Burning Chrome* (1986; 1988), William Gibson's collection of short stories, where he describes the SF written in the 1970s as 'confused, self-involved and stale'.[11] Despite, and perhaps because of, these omissions, it is hard not to recognise that feminist science fiction has had an undeniable impact on cyberpunk, both in its refusal to accept the generic limitations of this traditionally masculine genre, and in its concern to reframe the relationship between technology and social and sexual relations.

Cyberpunk explores the interface between human and machine in order to focus on the general question of what it means to be human; feminist science fiction has also explored that interface, but in order to challenge those universal and essentialist metaphors about 'humanity' which avoid confronting existing and unequal power relations. Cyberpunks and cyborgs can therefore be regarded as related responses to technology that are rooted in gender, and in different ways both seem to gesture towards possibilities for self-definition that move beyond existing sets of social and political relations. Before this can be considered in any detail, it is necessary to establish the extent to which cyberpunk's depiction of 'a future that is recognizably and painstakingly drawn from the modern condition'[12] constitutes a genuinely oppositional critique of the dominant culture and ideology. For the purposes of this discussion, the focus will be primarily on the work of William Gibson, since his writing articulates with particular clarity postmodern anxieties about the collapse of the real into the imaginary, and other kinds of 'inwardly collapsing hierarchies'.[13]

The confrontational relationship of cyberpunk to the genre as a whole is a partial expression of this 'collapse'; not only do cyberpunk writers acknowledge the influence of non-genre writers, but they are also prodigious appropriators of devices from other genres. At the same time, mainstream fiction has made increasing use of the metaphors and rhetoric of science fiction. The active involvement of cyberpunk in the erosion of cultural boundaries has generated an assumption that it also constitutes a radical response to the political conservativism of the 1980s by 'providing a language and metaphorical framework that will encourage the streets to speak'.[14] The heralding of cyberpunk as a kind of avant-garde 'movement' with its own manifesto has emphasised the implicitly radical sounding overtones of cyberpunk, which are based on an appropriation of the language of dissent contained in the street-wise posture and vocabulary of both punk and rock and roll. Bruce Sterling, however, has a clearer understanding of the position of cyberpunk and he carefully locates it within the traditions of science fiction:

> Cyberpunk is a natural extension of elements already present in science fiction, elements sometimes buried but always seething with potential. Cyberpunk has risen from within the SF genre; it is not an invasion but a modern reform.[15]

He makes a similar point when describing Gibson not as 'a table-pounding revolutionary, but a practical, hands-on retrofitter'.[16] The radicalism of cyberpunk does not lie in the unmediated expression of political dissent but in its capacity to render with considerable precision the sensuous surface detail of contemporary postmodern and post-industrial culture, through what Gibson calls the 'super-specificity' of the text.[17]

The profound sense of disequilibrium produced by the effects of new technology and transnational corporate capitalism is articulated in narratives that are themselves linguistically unstable. The eclecticism of *Neuromancer*, with its multiplicity of references to other genres combined with the rhetoric of information technology, has often been commented on. The most striking aspect of cyberpunk, however, is its knowing and ironic extrapolation from present trends to produce 'credible' futures, fictional landscapes that are ironic and playful, both in their simulation of surface reality and in their apparent effacement of the boundaries between inner and outer worlds. Veronica Hollinger has suggested that 'cyberpunk landscape tends to be choked with the debris of both language and objects; as a sign-system, it is overdetermined by a proliferation of surface detail which emphasizes the "outside" over the "inside".'[18] In its preoccupation with style, with the sign itself rather than the referent, cyberpunk has reworked the spatial and temporal dislocation that is the most characteristic feature of science fiction, collapsing the imaginary distance between the present and the future, the 'inside' and the 'outside'. It thus becomes part of what Istvan Csicsery-Ronay has called 'the SF of implosion',[19] in which the critical distance between appearance and reality has disappeared.

The effect of this collapse is ambiguous: for Pam Rosenthal, for example, it has the positive virtue of enabling cyberpunk to adopt a suitably street-wise and critical posture that she describes as the 'nonchalance of cyberpunk toward the bad new future that is upon us'.[20] The ironic detachment of cyberpunk enables it to gesture, however tentatively, to collective and cultural possiblities for communication and interaction which challenge the global information networks of multinational capitalism. In this sense, cyberpunk's negative critique can be regarded as the expression of a properly utopian moment in contemporary science fiction. For Fredric Jameson, on the other hand, the collapse of the future into the present represents 'an ultimate historicist breakdown in which we can no longer imagine the future at all, under any form – Utopian or catastrophic'.[21] In other words, the possibility of being able to achieve a sense of critical distance from the present, particularly by seeing the present as history, has been almost entirely eroded. Thus, cyberpunk's insistence on its 'credible futures' is, for Jameson, symptomatic of the postmodern denial of utopian aspiration that results from the loss of a sense of history. From this point of view, it is not possible to see in cyberpunk any kind of oppositional stance to the dominant ideology, and its narratives have to be seen as merely participating in a process by which reality and its imaginary representation are depicted as having become one and the same.

Bruce Sterling's claim that cyberpunks 'are perhaps the first SF generation to grow up not only within the literary tradition of science fiction but in a truly science-fictional world'[22] would seem to support such a view. The complex social and political relations of cultural production have been occluded here by the collapse of the boundaries between science fiction and reality. The description of the 'science fictional' nature of the world denies the neccessity for any critical distance between the fiction and the material conditions of its own existence. Cyberpunk's oppositional capacity is undoubtedly limited because of its unquestioning identification with those conditions, which is why it has become a readily available metaphor for use across almost the whole of the socio-cultural sphere. Cyberpunk's concern to delineate the 'almost-present' of its credible futures is, however, double-edged; on the one hand, it undermines its specificity as science fiction, and therefore its ability to make critical judgements on the culture in which it finds itself is compromised. On the other hand, the representation of a near future can function as a historical judgement on the present, and cyberpunk clearly understands the way in which the new socio-economic configurations of corporate capitalism are deeply embedded in our culture. This is why cyberpunk has been represented as being at the cutting edge of culture, defined by Lucius Shepard as that 'relating to the revolutionary, to outrage and revulsion with The Way Things Are, to the desire for renewal and change'.[23]

Despite the obvious limitations of cyberpunk's counter-cultural pretensions, its singular appropriateness to the contemporary postmodern environment suggests that the narratives do more than simply express the 'requisite attitude for the politically cynical struggling to survive in a decade driven by commercial avarice', as Andrew Ross puts it.[24] The way in which cyberpunk has been able to move out from the confines of science fiction into a whole range of other cultural productions including performance art, film and video, suggests that what is being challenged in cyberpunk is the social 'space' of science fiction itself. This links it in a most interesting way with feminist science fiction, which made its own, earlier challenge to that territory, and as a consequence, it has been able to sit much more loosely within the genre. Although the relationship of feminist science fiction both to technology and to the male-dominated 'hard' science tradition of science fiction is problematic, the relationship of cyberpunk to that tradition is far less problematic; indeed Veronica Hollinger has described cyberpunk as 'a product of the commercial mass market of "hard" SF'.[25] The small group of writers who have been chiefly associated with the 'urban fantasies' of cyberpunk are, unsurprisingly, predominantly white males (Pat Cadigan is the significant exception), and cyberpunk as a whole has been categorised as a 'baroque edifice of adolescent male fantasies'.[26] Timothy Leary's definition of cyberpunks as 'mavericks', 'loners' and 'smart alecks'[27] certainly supports this description: his list of proto-cyberpunks includes Prometheus, Christopher Columbus and Charles Augustus Lindbergh, not to mention the inevitable adolescent white male hacker such as the hero of the film *Wargames* who outmanoeuvres the computer that is about to start World War III.

The main characters in cyberpunk narratives are the hackers, transformed into street-wise rock 'n' roll heroes who wear mirrorshades and do 'biz' in the urban sprawl, dealing in designer drugs, information technology and stolen data, jacking into the matrix of cyberspace by means of implanted cranial sockets. Redefined in the role of computer cowboy, the cyberpunk hacker challenges the domination of the multinational corporations, deliberately recalling the actions of other mythic outsiders such as the hard-boiled detective. The comparison is necessarily a limited one, however, since cyberpunk is not anchored in the same set of social and political perspectives as those informing the detective genre. In many ways the cyberpunk hacker is the postmodern equivalent of the quintessential flâneur, strolling anonymously and heroically through the new physical and social spaces of the modern city streets. However, as Janet Wolff has pointed out, those particular urban spaces were not represented as being available to women in the same way, and it was not possible for there to be a female equivalent of the flâneur, a flâneuse.[28] In the modern city, 'respectable' women were forced to retreat from the public world of the city streets to the private world of the suburbs, and the public spaces that were to become increasingly available to women were the new department stores. The city has largely remained the traditional social space of the masculine, and the physical and psychic division between public and private, masculine and feminine, continues to be lived out in a postmodern environment of urban sprawl and inner-city decay.

The street culture of hustle and alienation so vividly evoked in William Gibson's narratives is drawn from the depiction of the 'mean streets' of hard-boiled detective fiction, those paradoxical spaces in which women were threatened by but also functioned as a threat to masculinity. What is interesting about Gibson's texts is that the sharp geographical and moral distinctions made in detective narratives between city centre and suburban areas, inner and outer, private and public are obliterated. The social spaces of masculinity and femininity have traditionally been defined by such distinctions, but the borderless urban environment of cyberpunk allows them to be called into question in a way that suggests the description of cyberpunk as 'boystown' is too superficial. In Gibson's narratives the mean streets have been transformed into an amorphous urban territory symbolised by the Sprawl, stretching from Boston to Atlanta and described, suitably enough, in terms of data: 'Program a map to display frequency of data exchange, every thousand megabytes a single pixel on a very large screen. Manhattan and Atlanta burn solid white.'[29] Other features of Gibson's narratives such as the celebration of consumerism may well conceal a more ambivalent attitude towards gender than would at first appear to be the case. Gibson often uses the image of the mall to convey the nature of the urban environment: 'Summer in the Sprawl, the mall crowds swaying like windblown grass, a field of flesh shot through with sudden eddies of need and gratification.'[30] In the ceaseless activity of this environment, 'the flow was pleasure',[31] but in its other aspect it is also 'like a deranged experiment in social Darwinism, designed by a bored researcher who kept one thumb permanently on the fast-forward button'.[32]

The overcrowded, decentred and fragmented territory of cyberpunk is presented as being endlessly and exhilaratingly busy in its dedication to the unifying principle of consumerism. Although Gibson's narratives convey an undeniable enjoyment at what he has called the 'sense of bustling commerce',[33] they do not present a straightforward account of social relations mediated through consumerism. Instead, cyberpunk parodies the mean streets of hard-boiled detective fiction by presenting them as the familiar spectacle of the shopping centre. These are the public spaces that modernis-ation made available to women, and so the streets in cyberpunk have acquired a quite different set of connotations which are super-imposed onto the connotations carried by the references to hard-boiled fiction. The female characters in Gibson's fiction, such as the prosthetically enhanced mercenary Molly Millions, borrowed from the character of Jael in Joanna Russ's *The Female Man*, inhabit this contradictory territory with ease. In the borderless territory of the Sprawl, women have the liberty to act because cyberpunk narratives undermine the opposition between private and public spheres. The Sprawl is therefore a feminised spatial metaphor in a way that the other central metaphor of cyberpunk – cyberspace – is not. This suggests that cyberpunk has a more complex relation to the politics of gender than has so far been acknowledged.

Just as Gibson's narratives both pay homage to and parody the mean streets of hard-boiled fiction, the process of commodification is obliquely criticised through the key totem of 'gomi' or junk. Accumulations of displaced objects are jumbled together in a parody of consumerism throughout Gibson's narratives, as in the following example from *Count Zero* (1986; 1987):

> Turner and Angela Mitchell made their way along the broken sidewalks to Dupont Circle and the station. There were drums in the Circle, and someone had lit a trash fire in the giant's marble goblet at the centre. Silent figures sat beside spread blankets as they passed, the blankets arrayed with surreal assortments of merchandise:the damp-swollen cardboard covers of black plastic audio discs beside battered prosthetic limbs trailing crude nerve-jacks, a dusty glass fishbowl filled with oblong steel dogtags, rubber-banded stacks of faded postcards, cheap Indo trodes still sealed in wholesaler's plastic, mismatched ceramic salt-and-pepper sets, a golf club with a peeling leather grip, Swiss army knives with missing blades, a dented tin wastebasket lithographed with the face of a President whose name Turner could almost remember (Carter? Grosvenor?), fuzzy holo-grams of the Monument . . .[34]

The new spaces of the postmodern global urban environment are literally built on gomi:

> Thirty-five percent of the landmass of Tokyo was built on gomi, on level tracts reclaimed from the Bay through a century's systematic

dumping. Gomi, there, was a resource to be managed, to be collected, sorted, carefully plowed under.

London's relationship to gomi was more subtle, more oblique. To Kumiko's eyes, the bulk of the city *consisted* of gomi. . . .

Gomi in the Sprawl was something else: a rich humus, a decay that sprouted prodigies in steel and polymer.[35]

A similar emphasis has been noted by Vivian Sobchak in an analysis of recent SF films:

The junkyard, the city dump, the trashy edges of town are culturally reinscribed as an *exotic* urban space that eroticizes and fetishizes material culture, that is valued for its marvelously unselective acquisitive power, its expansive capacity to accumulate, consume, and contain 'things', *any* thing, and its existential status as irrefutable testimony to the success of material production.[36]

Sobchak's view is informed by Fredric Jameson's account of the 'strange new hallucinatory exhilaration' of postmodern city life, whereby 'urban squalor can be a delight to the eyes, when expressed in commodification'.[37] The process of commodification described here is reminiscent of the notion of consumerism as false consciousness, by means of which differences of race, class and gender are effaced through the eroticism of consumption. The density of surface detail in Gibson's stories undoubtedly conveys some of this 'hallucinatory splendor' and Gibson himself has referred to what he calls the 'sexuality of junk'.[38] However, the narratives also convey a strong sense of irony at the notion that 'carefully sorted gomi' should be the undisputed sign of the contemporary, where high technology co-exists with 'garbage, kipple, refuse, the sea of cast-off goods our century floats on'.[39] The ironic detatchment of cyberpunk, its 'nonchalence' towards a high-tech future, can be more appropriately ascribed to what Peter Sloterdijk has called 'enlightened false consciousness'[40] a term that accurately describes the ambiguous tone of cyberpunk, critical of what it appears to be celebrating, but also appreciative of that towards which it is most critical. It is the very knowingness of cyberpunk texts that enables them to express a certain resistance to that 'negative futurism' to which both Sobchak and Jameson subscribe.

The limits of this resistance become more obvious, however, when the metaphor of cyberspace is considered. The feminisation of space achieved in the ironic and playful geography of cyberpunk's urban sprawl is not to be found in the homogeneous environment of cyberspace. Just as cyberpunk took on wider cultural connotations than those associated with the fictional worlds created by Gibson and other writers, so cyberspace has become part of an ever-widening discourse which celebrates the anticipated pleasures of virtual reality. The fledgling technology of virtual reality – electronic stereo vision helmets and data gloves – seeks to provide an entry into what Gibson has called the 'consensual hallucination' of cyberspace. The electronically constituted virtual reality of cyberspace articulates the contradictory fear of and fascination for technologies which actively participate in the breakdown of the boundaries between organic and inorganic, human and machine. Claudia Springer suggests that this breakdown 'involves transforming the self into something entirely new, combining technological with human identity',[41] a process which opens up radical possibilities for the breakdown of gender and other identities as part of a transformative social and political process such as that described by Donna Haraway in her 'Manifesto for cyborgs'.

In fact, these possibilities are never realised, as least not in cyberpunk narratives, because the social and temporal experience of cyberspace is centrally concerned with individual transcendence rather than transformation, with escape from social reality rather than engagement with it. Cyberspace is a vehicle for allowing the fluidity of social and sexual relations to be confined within the rationalist configurations of information technology, as Larry McCaffery unintentionally makes clear when he comments that Gibson's work raises the issue of 'the way information . . . not only controls our daily lives but may be the best way for us to undestand the fundamental processes that control the universe's ongoing transformations'.[42] Interface with the computer fulfils the desire to escape from the confines of the body, which, in Gibson's novels, is largely a masculine concern. In *Neuromancer*, for example, the 'permanent adrenaline high' experienced by Case comes from the fact that he spends his time 'jacked into a custom cyberspace deck that projected his disembodied consciousness into the consensual hallucination that was the matrix'. Once jacked into the 'bodiless exultation of cyberspace', the body becomes mere 'meat' for which computer cowboys profess a 'certain relaxed contempt' (12). Cyberspace, then, is a metaphor which expresses a fundamental ambivalence towards the body which is never textually resolved, particularly since sexual pleasure is defined principally in terms of an interaction with technology. As Claudia Springer suggests: 'Instead of losing our consciousness and experiencing bodily pleasures, cyborg imagery in popular culture invites us to experience sexuality by losing our bodies and becoming pure consciousness.'[43]

The 'consensual hallucination' of cyberspace blurs the boundaries between reality and simulation, self and other, thereby calling identity into question. It has the potential to be a new and heterogeneous space of desire, but because it remains dominated by the masculine, albeit in a sometimes contradictory relation to it, cyberspace becomes a place in which loss of identity is to be feared. In their preoccupation with the interface between human and machine, cyberpunk narratives reveal a deep anxiety about the disintegration of the unitary self and definitions of masculinity. Something of this is hinted at in Bruce Sterling's description of the central themes of cyberpunk: 'The theme of body invasion: prosthetic limbs, implanted circuitry, cosmetic surgery, genetic alteration. The even more powerful theme of mind-invasion: brain-computer interfaces, artificial intelligence, neurochemistry – techniques radically redefining the nature of humanity, the nature of the self.'[44] The use of terms like 'body invasion' and 'mind invasion' suggests uncertainty about the intimately intrusive power of the technology, since it poses above all potential threat to a stable masculine identity. At the same time, the list of technological processes is clearly designed to operate as a celebration of the technological sublime. The metaphysical overtones of cyberpunk technophilia, have been commented on by Samuel Delany:

> Religion rumbles all over the place in Gibson, just below the surface of the text: cyberspace is haunted by creatures just a step away from Godhood. And religious parallels begin to rumble through his plots almost everywhere we turn. The hard edges of Gibson's dehumanized technologies hide a residing mysticism.[45]

Cyberspace is populated by artificial intelligences (AIs) that control and manipulate the actions of the humans who enter cyberspace in order to facilitate their own merging. Human agency is usurped by the AIs but the 'almost permanent adrenaline high' of cyberspace is seen as reward enough in itself. In *Neuromancer*, the AIs Wintermute and Neuromancer merge to become the entire matrix, and Case, reasonably enough, asks at the end of the novel:

'So what's the score? How are things different? You running the world now? You God?' (316). Similarly, in *Mona Lisa Overdrive*, which is the final novel in Gibson's cyberpunk trilogy, the central characters play out most of their narrative existence in cyberspace, their human subjectivities translated into data, within a matrix which has become sentient, but which now seeks others of its own kind:

> 'You see', Colin said, brushing aside his brown forelock, a gesture like a schoolboy's in some antique play, 'when the matrix attained sentience, it simultaneously became aware of *another* matrix, another sentience.'
> 'I don't understand', she said, 'If cyberspace consists of the sum total of data in the human system. . . .'
> 'Yeah', the Finn said, turning out on to the long straight empty highway, 'but nobody's talkin' *human*, see?' (315)

In the text, the artificial intelligence previously known as Wintermute has become all-powerful, the ultimate patriarch, and in so doing it has achieved a kind of mystical 'Oneness'. Human consciousness has become an integral part of that unity, subject to the rule of the Father. In an interview, during which she returns to the issue of the potential of the boundary breakdowns between human and machine, Donna Haraway emphasises that any mystical unity, or 'Oneness' between human and machine intelligence can only replicate the kind of metaphysics of science that she was opposing in 'The manifesto for cyborgs': 'Any transcendentalist move is deadly; it produces death, through the fear of it. These holistic, transcendentalist moves promise a way out of history, a way of participating in the God trick.'[46]

Cyberspace is, then, a homogeneous space in which social processes are merely simulated: questions of identity and difference, and of the possibility of different relations to technology, are repressed. These repressions indicate that gender is indeed a key 'semiotic ghost' in cyberpunk. Perhaps this is why so many of the male characters in Gibson's work choose the thrill of the interface in preference to human relations, only able to relate to others in terms of data. The sexuality implicit in the masculine interface with computers is given ironic recognition by Gibson's use of the term 'jacked in', but the extent to which the texts are marked by the repression of difference is not given equal recognition. If Gibson's work can be cited as quintessential cyberpunk, then it would seem to be the case that cyberpunk is able to make only the most tentative of gestures towards the rethinking of gender relations. Characters like Molly Millions or even Laura, Bruce Sterling's heroine from the 'professional–managerial class' in his novel *Islands in the Net* (1988), are indicative of the presence and influence of feminist SF, but they cannot be said to be an expression of cyberpunk's own willingness to tackle questions of gender identity and subjectivity.

Despite large claims that cyberpunk has a 'surrealist perspective that revels in the deformation and destruction, the resurrection and reformation, of the human',[47] the narratives do not respond to the implicit invitation to reconsider the construction of human subjectivity, preferring instead to restate notions of the self in terms of a technology which continues to privilege the masculine. The deconstructive impulse of both feminism and postmodernism is circumscribed in cyberpunk by an unwillingness to go beyond the limitations of the existing social and political relations of technology. The radical possibilities of a new cybernetic order in which alternative versions of subjectivity and identity can emerge, are merely hinted at, but not pursued.

Pat Cadigan: Explorations of the Interface

In contrast, there are several recent science fiction texts by women, informed both by feminism and by the partially critical insights of cyberpunk, that do attempt to explore the implications for subjectivity and social relations that are implicit in cyberpunk. The pseudo-mystical version of the human–machine interface that dominates male cyberpunk is rejected in favour of explorations of the human and social consequences of the interface. Pat Cadigan is currently one of the few women cyberpunk writers and is the only woman writer to be included in the cyberpunk anthology *Mirrorshades*. Her narratives try to avoid the kind of technological essentialism that surfaces in the narratives of a writer like Gibson, where a distinction is made between the high adrenaline, male-dominated world of cyberspace and the female-dominated, passive world of 'simstim' stars and direct-input soaps. Cadigan is more concerned to depict the human–machine interface as a complex environment of negative and exploitative possibilities as well as positive and potentially liberating ones.

In 'Pretty Boy Crossover', which is included in *Patterns* (1989; 1991), her own collection of short stories, Cadigan focuses on the relation between power and pleasure by ironically equating the male fascination with the interface with masculinity's fascination with itself. The main characters, Bobby and Pretty Boy, are young, beautiful, wholly egocentric and very hip. Such is Bobby's narcissistic pleasure in himself that he has accepted the option offered by an ever-hungry entertainment industry to 'go over', to become 'Self aware data'. By being imprinted on a microchip as 'sentient information', his youth and beauty are preserved for ever as 'pure video'. As long as his 'look' remains fashionable, Bobby will be shown as living video in the dance clubs, always there for the pleasure of others' gaze and for his own pleasure at being the object of their gaze. He has literally become the image of himself in order to become the object of desire. Pretty Boy, who loves Bobby, is offered the same option:

> We need to get you before you're twenty-five, before the brain stops growing. A mind taken from a still-growing brain will blossom and adapt . . . we'll be taking Pretty Boys for as long as they're publicly sought-after. It's the most efficient way to find the best performers, go for the ones everyone wants to see or be. The top of the trend is closest to heaven. And even if you never make a breakthrough, you'll still be entertainment. Not such a bad way to live for a Pretty Boy. Never have to age, to be sick, to lose touch.[48]

Pretty Boy's final refusal of the temptation to go over is less convincing than Bobby's obvious pleasure in his new existence as distilled information, but the story is interesting for the way in which it tentatively raises the question of human agency and identity in the interface with technology. Bobby embodies the essentialist fantasy of the autonomous masculine subject which has transcended all social and cultural restrictions by means of the interface. By becoming 'pure video', Bobby has completed the circle of masculine domination by becoming his own Other. In Cadigan's narrative, then, the interface is represented as a form of power and control, by means of which definitions of the human subject are reified.

The limitations of cyberpunk as a formal device for renegotiating a more developed sense of subjectivity become clear in Cadigan's ambiguously titled cyberpunk novel, *Synners* (1991). Cadigan's novel is an immensely detailed account of the subjective experience of life at the interface and it exemplifies what Bruce

Sterling calls cyberpunk's ability to 'carry extrapolation into the fabric of daily life'.[49] The post-earthquake, near-future Californian society depicted by Cadigan is chaotic and fragmented, and the technology of implants and human–computer interface is so ubiquitous that there appear to be few dangers associated with its use. It is an environment in which hacking has become a routine activity that is an accepted part of youth culture, the pleasures of virtual reality have been harnessed by the advertising industry, Los Angeles has attempted to solve its traffic problems by means of an intermittently successful system of computer-controlled rental cars, and various forms of mental illness and other imbalances in the nervous system are stabilised through brain implants rather than drugs.

Although the novel contains as much technology as other cyberpunk writing, the mystique of the interface is absent because the technology has, in a sense, been domesticated by its own fictional environment. Cadigan's narrative suggests that it is precisely this sense of technology as mundane that has established a set of power relations that is increasingly threatening to individual and collective identity. However, those relations of power are not examined to any great extent beyond the suggestion that it is the transnational corporations that have a position of hegemonic control, and exactly who stands in opposition to those relations of power is left very vague. The central theme of the novel concerns the affects of the development of a new kind of interactive socket implant, made from living tissue, that will enable the brain both to receive and send information directly from another brain. The problems facing the corporation that is developing the brain socket are summed up by one of the characters in terms of public acceptability rather than accountability:

> I still say you're gonna have to go some fucking distance to turn public opinion on what looks like a faster, easier way of mind control and brainwashing, all that shit. There's still plenty of people around who believe that manic-depressives and the schizos and the migrainers and the epileptics and the narcoleptics and *all* those leptics are morally wrong to have little buttons in their heads to keep them even. Hell, there's still plenty that think test-tube babies are a fucking atrocity. (69)

Cadigan describes a society saturated with technology that is somehow 'out of control'. The notion that technology is out of control is mentioned several times, and, while it corresponds to the generally fragmented social and cultural environment of the narrative, it also suggests that Cadigan is not satisfied with the often uncritical celebration of technology that is characteristic of cyberpunk. The 'synners' of the title are a double-edged reference to both the technology and its lack of accountability. Synners are the video artists who use the technology of virtual reality to synthesise images and rock music into visually powerful music videos. The experimental brain sockets are to be used in the first instance to transmit these images direct from the imagination of the synthesisers to the mass-market consumer. The connotations of the term 'synners' also indicates that Cadigan is interested in the moral dimensions of corporate decision making concerning the application of technology, an interest she shares more with Bruce Sterling than Gibson. As one of the characters in *Synners* suggests:

> Knowledge is power. But power corrupts. Which means the Age of Fast Information is an extremely corrupt age in which to live.
> 'Aren't they all?' Sam asked him.
> He smiled his dreamy little smile at her. 'Ah, but I think we're approaching a kind of corruption unlike anything we've ever known before, Sam-I-Am. Sometimes I think we may be on the verge of an original sin.' (53)

Although Cadigan does not present the human–machine interface entirely in terms of the 'residing mysticism' of Gibson's narratives, nevertheless the cyberpunk framework almost inevitably leads to the suggestion that the technology is capable of exerting its own hegemony over other systems of thought. Technology as 'sentient information' or artificial intelligence can then be thought of as constructing its own Other, over whom it seeks power.

Cadigan follows the pattern of Gibson's narratives by having a matrix that becomes sentient, although she does give it a sense of humour – it calls itself 'Art Fish', a joke which becomes clear if the name is said quickly. It also represents itself as unequivocally male. It is ultimately joined by a human intelligence in the form of the video artist, Visual Mark, who is the first synner to be given the experimental brain socket so that his creative ability to synthesise music and images can be sold on the mass market. The new technology gives Mark the chance to leave his ailing 'meat' for good and go permanently on-line:

> He lost all awareness of the meat that had been his prison for close

to fifty years, and the relief he felt at having laid his burden down was as great as himself. His *self*. And his *self* was getting greater all the time, both ways, greater as in more wonderful and greater as in bigger. (232)

Mark's 'self' eventually joins with Art to become 'Markt', thereby authenticating the assumed masculinity of the ubiquitous 'Art'. In the alliance of technology with masculinity that is central to cyberpunk, the metaphor of the interface is consistently used to establish 'masculinity' as universal and hegemonic. Despite Cadigan's inclusion of a significant number of strong female characters who are central to the narrative, the depiction of women as other in cyberpunk goes unquestioned, resulting in a process described by Judith Butler, in which 'the universal person and the masculine gender are conflated, thereby defining women in terms of their sex and extolling men as the bearers of a body-transcendent universal personhood'.[50]

Cadigan's attempt to suggest an oppositional stance to existing relations of power is largely defeated by the reification of gender relations that is implicit in cyberpunk. The integration of human and artificial intelligence to produce a new configuration is an interesting attempt to go beyond the mysticism of the matrix, but it does not include gender in any significant way. The new identity of 'Markt' is not used to open up the question of identity generally, and it clearly leaves intact existing gender relations. In fact, gender relations are side-stepped by Cadigan, who concentrates instead on the more general question of relations between the organic and the inorganic through the central metaphor of synthesis. It is the presence of Mark's 'self' in the information net that provokes its almost total collapse, thus enabling the narrative to offer its moral critique of the uncontrolled application of technology. After he has been fitted with an experimental brain socket, Visual Mark's success at transmitting the images he visualises are enough to encourage the mass marketing of the sockets. It also gives Mark the opportunity to achieve his burning desire to join the reality of the matrix and provokes his decision to go permanently on-line.

While Mark is in the matrix he has a massive stroke, the effects of which he transmits directly to the brains of all those consumers who also have sockets. The stroke acts as an intelligent and voracious virus and destroys not only the brains of those with sockets but also the rest of the net. The virus is defeated by the combined forces of what remains of the human–machine interface, in other words by Markt and the hackers. The virtual collapse of the information system world-wide provides Cadigan with the narrative opportunity to make a point that is overlooked in cyberpunk's generally celebratory attitude towards technology – that it has in some way to become accountable. At the end of the novel one of the synners says: '"Think on this one. All *appropriate technology* hurt somebody. A whole lot of somebodies. Nuclear fission, fusion, the fucking Ford assembly line, the fucking airplane. *Fire*, for Christ's sake. Every technology has its original sin." She laughed. "Makes us original synners. And we still got to live with what we made"' (435). Notions of accountability suggest an interactive relationship to technology, one that is less concerned with personal power and control and more interested in social and collective responsibility.

Although this emphasis distinguishes Cadigan's version of cyberpunk from Gibson's and despite the presence of the active female characters in the narrative, and a corresponding absence of anxiety about the invasive nature of the technology, *Synners* nevertheless suggests that cyberpunk is fairly intractable as far as the representation of gender relations is concerned. Cadigan's metaphor of 'synthesis' allows her to explore the potential impact of the human–machine interface in terms of universals rather than in terms of specific social relations. Thus, the interface produces the 'synthesizing human and the synthesized human, all of us being the former, and Art Fish being the latter' (386). The radicalism of this new synthesis lies in its challenge to definitions of individuality and identity, but it is promptly confined within the familiar framework of masculinist assumptions about 'humanity', and questions of difference are redirected towards the problem of whether or not an artificial intelligence can be considered to be human. It would seem that cyberpunk is marked above all by an unresolved anxiety about gender relations, and that, despite its potentially radical insights into the possibilities of the interface, and its postmodern concern with subjectivity, it cannot escape from a predominantly patri- archal view of social relations, no matter how contradictory that view might be.

Cyborg Transgressions in the Work of Rebecca Ore, Marge Piercy and Elisabeth Vonarburg

Although cyberpunk exerted for a time a particular kind of cultural and masculinist hegemony over questions concerning the impact of information technology on social relations, this did not prevent those same questions being posed from outside the framework of cyberpunk. The writers discussed in the following section utilise the metaphor of the cyborg rather than that of cyberspace to examine the relationships of power that are concealed within and disguised by cybernetic systems. The cyborg metaphor emphasises the increasingly fluid borders between reality and simulation as definitions of the human as cyborg and the cyborg as human become blurred. Where the hyper-reality of cyberspace reifies existing social relations and power structures in its representation of near futures, the cyborg metaphor, by operating within the dynamic of 'permanently partial identities and contradictory standpoints',[51] seeks to confront them. The cyborg embodies the notion of transgression against the limits and controls of the cybernetic systems within which it is situated. Within the context of the unstable boundaries between the real and the simulated, human and cyborg, the question of identity becomes highly charged, because it can become a crucial means of contesting what Bill Nichols describes as the 'reification, the commodification, the patterns of mastery and control'[52] that are at the heart of contemporary cybernetic systems.

In the novels under discussion in this section, the disturbed and increasingly disturbing relationship between the real and the simulated is explored in terms of the replication of human life through genetic engineering. The narratives provide a situation in which definitions of what it means to be human can no longer be taken for granted and, if those definitions are in a state of flux, then the notion of having a fixed and 'natural' identity becomes problematic. What are often held to be the innate characteristics of masculinity and femininity are revealed to be cultural fictions. In presenting these issues, the narratives are able to challenge the idea that gender itself is a stable and unchanging given. Both Rebecca Ore's novel, *The Illegal Rebirth of Billy The Kid* (1991) and Marge Piercy's novel *Body of Glass* (1992), focus on the problem of how identity is defined at the point where the reality of the simulation and the simulation of reality intersect. Ore's Billy the Kid and Piercy's cyborg/Golem, are constructed from genetic material and programmed to behave in particular ways, but the question of whether or not they can be defined as human is central to both texts. Although Billy's genetic material is reconstituted from animal cells, he believes himself to be fully human, and the narrative deals with the contradiction between his own struggle to define himself as human and the cultural definition of him as a 'dog meat robot'.[53] Piercy's cyborg, Yod, is aware of himself as a cybernetic construction but is described in equally contradictory terms as 'Not a human person, but a person.'[54] These contradictions are signalled in a more visible way in the title chosen for the American publication of Piercy's book, *He, She and It*. The incoherence of these contradictory definitions is central to the narratives and it is deliberately left unresolved, a strategy that enables the question to be raised of the way in which the subject is constituted in culture.

Although both narratives are situated in familiar cyberpunk territory, they contain little of what George Slusser has called the 'sizzle and flash'[55] qualities of cyberpunk prose. Ore's writing in particular is remarkably flat and sparse and the high-tech environment of the narrative is deliberately understated. This places the narrative in a contradictory relation to the kind of overtly masculinist cyberpunk writing that is described by Bruce Sterling as 'the literary equivalent of the hard-rock "wall of sound"',[56] and allows Ore to explore cyberpunk's repressed anxieties about the nature of masculinity itself. Her depiction of the increasingly tenuous boundaries between the real and the simulated draws attention to the nature of all binary divisions, including that of gender. The issue of gender identity is contained within the question of what constitutes the human. Her narrative is populated both by 'real' humans and simulated humans who think they are real, and in such an ambiguous environment, the notion that identity is ontologically given is rendered problematic.

The loss of a clear sense of boundaries leads to uncertainty about identity, and this has particular resonances where gender is concerned. Ore's narrative explores this on two levels, through the identity confusion experienced by the Billy the Kid simulacrum, and through the ambivalent sexual attraction women feel towards his manufactured maleness. In other words, gender is absolutely implicated in any uncertainty about boundaries between the real and the simulated and, as the relations between the real and the simulated become increasingly insecure, attempts to depict gender as unproblematic become fraught with difficulty. Billy's dual existence as a simulacrum and as an object of desire means that he is denied the power that his masculinity could be expected to bestow on him. It is Billy's struggle to distinguish between his programmed masculinity and his own learned sense of gender that makes explicit the anxieties about masculinity that are implicit in cyberpunk.

Simulacra like Billy are made to be disposable, and they are used either as spies by government agencies, or as playthings for the rich. Simon Boyle, Billy's maker, works for the CIA in the secret world of 'chimera intelligence', an appropriate enough setting in a narrative which focuses on those areas of confusion which occur in the overlap between the real and the simulated. Simon Boyle has gone 'rogue' by illegally manufacturing Billy for use by wealthy female clients who want the experience of sex with a simulated killer from the nineteenth century. Boyle voyeuristically participates in every sexual encounter, because not only does he watch each one, but, in the guise of Pat Garrett, he also gets to shoot Billy dead afterwards. Billy is then revived by Boyle, minus the memory of the experience of his own death(s), for the next client. All Billy's memories are false, given to him by Boyle so that he can believe himself to be human, but the memories themselves are drawn from the multiplicity of mythical material surrounding the historical figure of Billy. 'Billy' is an image drawn from any number of other possible images, so that when he says 'I've been in dime novels all my life' (135), this is both literally and metaphorically true.

The particular images chosen by Simon Boyle to furnish Billy with a personality act as indicators of Boyle's own sexual doubts and obsessions, which are focused on Billy's body: '*When I kill him, I bring him back, like a god.* He liked that part, Pat Garrett treating Billy's gunshot wound, outside both Billy's history and his own' (18). The shooting itself is described in fairly obvious sexual terms: 'The gun Simon held was an exact replica, heavy against his thigh – *don't think this phallic bullshit* – a slight gleam on the barrel, worn trigger guard, the grip's open-pored grain all pointing at the cylinder, splinters smoothed away by handling and sweat' (19). Boyle has absolute power over Billy's body, he resurrects Billy's body each time he dies, washes his memory out and heals him. Boyle repeatedly constructs and deconstructs Billy as object, controlling what Billy can do or say by means of implants, and even controlling what he can see by making alterations to Billy's visual cortex. In the narrative, the metaphor of the cybernetic process is based on a masculinist definition of power which is constantly fearful of being undermined by the very confusion of boundaries in which it originated. Both Boyle and Billy are confined within this process, one as maker, the other as a thing that has been made. However, Billy's desire to overcome his conditioning as chimera acts as an alternative metaphor, one that suggests the importance of the attempt to restore human agency over cybernetic process.

When Billy is stolen from Boyle by one of his clients and subsequently escapes, the conditioning which has prevented Billy from understanding his actual environment begins to break down: the narrative present of 2067 leaks into his simulated nineteenth-century present and similarly, his existence as simulacrum is constantly compromised by his struggle to be human. Billy's ability to relearn, to reconstruct himself rather than be reprogrammed, is central to his increasingly complex social relations with humans, including that with Jane, his one-time protector who becomes his long-term lover. Their relationship begins to develop as he recognises and overcomes the programmed responses to women that he had as Billy the Kid. Jane in turn has to overcome her suspicion of his designed masculinity. Cybernetic conditioning here acts as a metaphor for all those gendered responses that are culturally constructed. It is only by recognising them that Billy can learn to understand and live the contradiction that he is a fully human chimera: 'His craving for a normal life was Simon's little joke then, but it kept Billy sane now' (302). Boyle, on the other hand, is eliminated by the CIA and, in a final irony, he is replaced by a simulacrum of himself which has no memory of the illegal creation of Billy.

Billy and Boyle, then, embody different versions of the masculine desire for power and autonomy which is implicit in cybernetic systems. Boyle's control over Billy's body, with its suggestion of sexual obsession, symbolises the dehumanising power of the processes over Boyle and the reification of all social relations. Billy's resistance to the definition of himself as a 'dog-meat robot' suggests that, on the contrary, definitions of reality and of the self are contingent rather than fixed, and that such definitions are in a constant process of negotiation. In other words, there is a necessary interaction between reality and simulation in cybernetic systems, just as there is in all cultural processes, which is somewhat at odds with Baudrillard's worst-case scenario in which the simulation replaces and destroys reality, even supposing there is a single version of reality which can be replaced.

The tension between the metaphor of the cyborg as product of controlling cybernetic processes and the metaphor of the cyborg as embodying resistance to that control is a major concern in Marge Piercy's *Body of Glass*. Piercy's novel is set in an increasingly familiar near future of corporate control, pollution and war. Vast areas of the world have been made largely uninhabitable and the great multinationals have built huge corporate domes on every continent to provide protected living space for their professional and technical employees. Everyone else lives outside the domes, either in the free towns which stubbornly maintain their independence from the multis, or in the Glop, Piercy's more radical version of Gibson's Sprawl. The political struggle between the multis and those who seek to resist their influence provides one of the main themes of the narrative; the other is the relationship between the cyborg, Yod, and the human, Shira, which is examined in the context of a more thoroughgoing critique of social and sexual relations than that attempted by Ore.

Shira is employed in cybernetics by the Yakamura-Stichen corporation, but has resigned and returned home to the free town of Tikva after custody of her son has been awarded to her husband by the corporation. Tikva and other free towns are under constant attack from assassins and information pirates sent by the corporations, and so a cyborg has been built in Tikva to protect the town. The corporations banned the production of cyborgs after the cyber-riots, which means that Yod's existence has to be kept as secret as possible, and Shira is asked to help him/it to learn how to pass as human. Yod's maker, Avram, has created him as male on the assumption that this will make him more 'human', as if it is masculinity, even in its cyborg form, which defines the capacity to be human:

> Avram looked slightly embarrassed. He did not look at Yod or at her but at the ceiling, his hands joining behind his back. 'I felt the more closely he resembled a human being, the less likely he would be detected. It will be necessary for him to pass time with humans, and he must seem as much like them as possible.' (68)

Shira's job is to continue to socialise Yod, taking up where her grandmother Malkah's interpersonal programming of Yod has left off. It is Malkah who has programmed into Yod what she calls 'some wild cards' (74) to counterbalance Avram's masculinist definition of the world, and it is these that enable him to form relationships with the people he was created to protect.

Yod's cyborg masculinity means that he occupies the unexpected narrative position of alien and outsider, and is therefore denied access to structures of power. Although Yod's programmed ability to learn increases his sense of himself as a subject separate from and often in conflict with Avram, whom he refers to ironically as 'Father', he does not have ultimate control over his own body because Avram has built a self-destruct command into the cyborg. Yod therefore occupies a contradictory position in the narrative, and Piercy uses his developing consciousness to question the way in which social and sexual relations are shaped by conventions and definitions that are thought of as fixed and natural. The narrative details the way in which the growth of Yod's self-awareness increases his desire to become fully involved in the community he is programmed to protect, and eventually leads to him becoming Shira's lover:

> I'm conscious of my existence. I think, I plan, I feel, I react. I consume nutrients and extract energy from them. I grow mentally, if not physically, but does the inability to become obese make me less alive? I feel the desire for companionship. If I can't reproduce, neither can many humans. (88)

Yod's list of characteristics is a demonstration that he thinks of himself as being 'alive', but throughout the narrative Piercy clearly distinguishes between the notion of being alive and actually being human. She does this by means of Yod's periodic self-examinations and also through the device of the parallel story in which Malkah tells Yod about the Golem in sixteenth-century Prague, created by mystical means from clay by the chief rabbi to protect the Jews in the ghetto. It/he is named Joseph, he thinks and feels, but he is not human and when the danger to the Jews has passed, his maker returns him to clay. The mythical nature of the golem is used to suggest that the contradiction at the heart of Yod's existence – that he is a person but not a 'human person' – is ultimately insurmountable, and this enables Piercy to relocate the question of identity within the metaphor of the human as cyborg, rather than the cyborg as human.

Yod's somewhat one-dimensional definition of himself as 'alive' is contrasted to the female characters in Piercy's narrative, who strive for a definition of the self which is both multiple and fluid, a recurring theme in Piercy's writing. The metaphor of the technological alteration of the body by means of implants, prostheses, and so on, signifies the possibility of achieving such a multiplicity, although the struggle to achieve it within the parameters of existing sets of relationships is depicted as being both difficult and painful. Shira's relationship with Yod demonstrates the pain and pleasure of the struggle, even though it is defined solely in terms of heterosexual identity. He frees her from her dependence on a former lover, helps her reclaim her son with whom he also establishes a close relationship, but he himself cannot survive since he has been programmed to protect Tikva, and that entails his own destruction. The text's utopian possibilities are not represented by Yod's cyborg masculinity, but by the female characters in the narrative, because they are defined as existing in opposition to gender expectations.

The power structures which embody those expectations are largely symbolised in the narrative by the corporations. Piercy links the political opposition to the corporations on the part of the central female characters to their equally oppositional relation to gender identity. She presents Malkah, for example, as a great grandmother who goes against the grain of cultural constructions of age in that she continues to be significantly involved both in her work and in social and sexual relationships. Her daughter, Riva, is Shira's mother, but her political opposition to the corporate monopoly on information was such that she gave up motherhood and became an information pirate, leaving Shira to be brought up by Malkah. Riva's lover and companion, Nili, has a genetically engineered and technologically enhanced body which both parodies and undermines the masculine defininition of cyborg. Nili is from a community of women which has the capacity to make and remake itself: 'We have no men. We clone and engineer genes. After birth we undergo additional alteration. We have created ourselves to endure, to survive, to hold our land' (187).

Although it is described in more casual terms and is less central to the narrative, the relationship between Nili and Riva acts as a critical parallel to that between Shira and Yod, since it is the only relationship that is not defined either in heterosexual terms or in terms of dependency. The capacity for transformation represented

by Nili provides a key metaphor for the kinds of positive changes
that cybernetic systems have the potential to produce, particularly
for women, once the binary divide between nature and culture has
been challenged. Yod's cyborg existence is ultimately determined by
the masculine hegemony implicit in cybernetic systems, but Nili
represents the possibility of transgressing the predefined boundaries
and limits on identity imposed by that particular cybernetic model.

Piercy uses the problematic nature of the cyborg to provide a
generalised critique of dominant cultural notions of human identity
which, when they are embedded in cybernetic systems, reproduce
existing structures of power. Her analysis of the gendered nature of
constructions of identity goes further than that of either Cadigan or
Ore, because she has recognised that the metaphor of the human–
machine interface is itself gendered, hence the significant differences
in the definitions of Yod and Nili as cyborgs. However, despite the
fact that the utopian possibilities of the text lie firmly with the
feminine, the implications for women of a cyborg identity are not,
in the end, fully explored. Despite the narrative refusal to endorse
Yod's cyborg version of masculinity, the question of identity is
framed too often in terms of the masculine because of the insistent
focus on Yod's sense of self, rather than, say, that of Nili. Yod is an
all too literal embodiment of a cyborg, which significantly
undermines the power of Donna Haraway's original metaphor of
the cyborg identity, even though Piercy herself acknowledges the
influence of the essay in which the metaphor appears. The narrative
development of alternative relations to cybernetic systems through
the metaphor of the cyborg remains, finally, somewhat limited in
Piercy's novel.

The way in which the erosion of boundaries impacts on
definitions of gender is central to Elisabeth Vonarburg's novel, *The
Silent City*. Strictly speaking, this is a pre-cyberpunk novel, since the
original French version was published in 1981, although the English
translation appeared in 1988. Despite the fact that this was also
before the publication of Haraway's 'A manifesto for cyborgs', the
cyborg metaphor and its capacity to suggest new and oppositional
identities is the subject of the narrative. The narrative focuses on the
female body as the primary site on which the contradictions of
gender identity are played out, in the context of the shifting borders
between the human as cyborg and the cyborg as human. Vonarburg
uses the metaphor of metamorphosis of the body to suggest that

existing dualisms of nature and culture, self and other, insider and outsider are instrumental in defining gender in terms of relations of dominance and subordination. Subjectivity is therefore constructed according to the ideological requirements of these relations, giving an illusory coherence to what is actually a contingent ordering of reality. However, the instability of identity, and the instability in the relation between the real and the simulated that is implicit in cybernetic systems, undermines that illusory coherence by creating multiple possibilities for alternative orderings of reality and constructions of subjectivity.

The narrative is set in a far future, rather than in the provocatively near future of cyberpunk. In the distant past of this future, technologically complex cities were built underground to provide the privileged and powerful with protection from the effects of war, famine, pollution and the climatic change which eventually devastated the world. In a familiar metaphor establishing the subordinate relation of 'outsider' to 'insider', everyone else is condemned to remain Outside, and the narrative is concerned with the effects of this hierarchy of social relations on both the City and the Outside. Despite the fact that the Cities have the sophisticated cybernetic technologies of genetic engineering, including gene banks and rejuvenation treatments, the populations within the Cities have dwindled, becoming increasingly insular and almost completely isolated from the 'Outside'. As the few survivors become too old or disinterested to socialise, they move vicariously about the City by means of robotic simulacra of themselves, or even of other people, which they control and through which they see and speak to others.

Communication is achieved either through these simulacra or through the network of screens throughout the City that are linked into the central computer system. Everything that happens in the City is recorded, via the screens or the eyes of the simulacra, so that any moment in the past is always available to the present as a simulated reality. As the boundaries between the real and the simulated become unstable, so also do the distinctions between appearance and reality, the past and the present. This blurring of boundaries establishes the narrative conditions within which social and sexual relations and definitions of identity can be depicted as contingent rather than fixed.

The focus for Vonarburg's discussion of these issues in the narrative is Elisa, a human embryo cybernetically produced and

brought to term by Paul, one of the last survivors in the City. She is
the successful outcome of years of haphazard and brutal genetic
experiments that Paul has conducted on countless unwilling subjects
drawn from the Outside. His 'Project' is to stabilise a potentially
auto-regenerative gene that he has discovered in some of the
Outsiders, in order to develop 'A new race capable of surviving in a
transformed world. Human beings who won't be afraid of wounds,
illness, or radiation. Cellular regeneration, and in the final analysis,
total mastery of the life process' (18). The narrative development
makes it clear that Paul's use of technology is not disinterested, but
is irrevocably tied to his masculinity, with the result that the
dominant relations of technology are expressed in terms of
masculine power over and control of knowledge.

Elisa is a success in Paul's terms because she can regenerate her
own cells, but the additional factor in her genetically engineered
abilities is that she can alter the shape and gender of her body. As
female, and as the progeny of Paul's Project, Elisa is therefore subject
to a double set of constraints which emphasise control and
hierarchy. However, her ability to change her gender means that she
is always in potential conflict with those constraints, rather than
being subordinate to them. Since Elisa is not narratively held within
a subordinate position by her gender, she can represent an
alternative and oppositional definition of cybernetic systems, in
which the repressive rhetoric of 'mastery and control' is replaced by
more emancipatory and fluid possibilities.

The first part of the narrative depicts Elisa's struggle to
challenge Paul's control over her, which ends when she kills him.
Their relationship is a parody of that betweeen father and child,
where authority resides as much in the technology as it does in
Paul. In this ambiguously incestuous relationship, Paul's control
of the technological processes which produced Elisa is equated
with control over her body. Her body is therefore the object of desire
as both woman and process, a symbolic conflation in which her
body becomes a signifier for the masculine hegemony of cybernetic
systems. However, Elisa's capacity for complete bodily metamorphosis means that she cannot be fixed as female within
this signifying system, and she therefore poses a threat to that
hegemony. In the narrative she escapes from Paul's control by
metamorphosing into Hansa, who is male, and leaves the City for
the Outside. This has far-reaching effects in narrative terms, since it

ultimately results in the collapse of the barriers between City and Outside.

Gender metamorphosis is a useful narrative manoeuvre which enables Vonarburg to explore the precariousness of sexual identity and the potential that lies in the dissolution of divisions between physical and psychic boundaries. As Hanse, Elisa makes love to Judith, who sees her as male:

> I understand you so well and I love you and it doesn't matter if my body isn't really my body, what does it mean isn't my body, it's *me* it's me Elisa Hanse no matter what body I am myself and pleasure is pleasure that's all love is love. (93)

The dissolution of textual features in this passage conveys the fluid and shifting nature of Elisa's sexual embodiment, and if the body itself can no longer be regarded as a stable boundary, then other binary divisions become equally hard to sustain. Elisa's cyborg identity expresses the potential for change that such instability contains. There is, however, an unresolved tension in the narrative between the metaphor of gender metamorphosis and the cybernetics of reproductive technology, and the 'Project' becomes the focal point of this tension.

In the final part of the narrative, Elisa takes up the Project again, and produces several generations of children who all possess her ability to metamorphose. Her intention is that these children should mix their genetic inheritance randomly with that of the Outsiders, with unknowable but hopeful consequences. Despite the open-ended intention of the narrative, the metaphor of the Project is suffused with connotations of technological determinism: it is situated within the negative politics of artificial reproduction, whereby control over reproductive processes is removed from women by a male-dominated scientific and technological system. Vonarburg fails to give the Project a context other than that of Paul's original genetic ambitions, and despite Elisa's personal vision, it remains embedded in those negative politics. It is at odds with the quite different politics implied by the metaphor of gender metamorphosis, in which possibilities for the redefinition of gender identity and social relations are explored. In the end, Vonarburg's text remains disappointingly unclear about exactly where the narrative emphasis should lie.

Each of the writers discussed in this section has been concerned with the complex and contradictory relations of domination in cybernetic systems. They have sought to engage with the kinds of issues raised by cyberpunk, while challenging the manifest anxieties of this 'vanguard white male art'[57] about the instability of boundaries and categories. While the dystopian near future of cyberpunk has an undeniable frisson, its version of the social relations of technology offers little opportunity for the redefinitions envisioned by Haraway's cyborg metaphor. However, the cyborg texts, despite their contradictions and ambiguities, do contain a critique of the masculine hegemony of cybernetic systems which examines their impact on gender and identity, and asks whether those systems are capable of sustaining other sets of relations and meanings.

Notes

1 Intersections

1. Donna Haraway, 'The promises of monsters: A regenerative politics for inappropiate/d others', in Lawrence Grossberg, Cary Nelson, Paula Treichler (eds), *Cultural Studies* (New York and London, Routledge, 1992), p. 300.
2. Donna Haraway, 'A manifesto for cyborgs: Science, technology, and socialist feminism in the 1980s', *Socialist Review*, Part 80 (1985), p. 66.
3. For substantial accounts of the history of science fiction, see Brian Aldiss, with David Wingrove, *Trillion Year Spree* (London, Gollancz, 1986); Paul A. Carter, *The Creation of Tomorrow: Fifty years of magazine science fiction* (New York, Columbia University Press, 1977); for a theoretical account of the genre, see Darko Suvin, *Metamorphoses of Science Fiction: On the poetics and history of a literary genre* (New Haven and London, Yale University Press, 1979).
4. Andreas Huyssen, *After the Great Divide: Modernism, mass culture, postmodernism* (Bloomington, Indiana University Press, 1986), p. 216.
5. Brian McHale, *Postmodernist Fiction* (London and New York, Methuen), 1987, pp. 68–9.
6. *ibid.*, pp. 62 and 65,
7. Peter Brooker, *Modernism/ Postmodernism* (London and New York, 1992), p. 20.
8. Roger Luckhurst, 'Border policing: Postmodernism and science fiction', *Science Fiction Studies*, 18 (1991), p. 365.
9. Fredric Jameson, 'Progress versus utopia; or, can we imagine the future?', *Science Fiction Studies*, 9, Part 2 (1982), p. 153.
10. David Harvey, *The Condition of Postmodernity* (Oxford, Basil Blackwell, 1989), p. 328.

139

11. Fredric Jameson, 'The politics of theory: Ideological positions in the postmodern debate', *New German Critique*, 33 (1984), p. 63.

12. Fredric Jameson, *Postmodernism, or, the Cultural Logic of Late Capitalism* (London and New York, verso, 1991), p. 26.

13. Fredric Jameson, 'Postmodernism and consumer society', in Hal Foster (ed.), *Postmodern Culture* (London, Pluto, 1985), p. 125.

14. Jacqueline Rose, '*The Man who Mistook his Wife for a Hat* or *A Wife is Like an Umbrella* – fantasies of the modern and postmodern', in Andrew Ross (ed.), *Universal Abandon? The politics of postmodernism* (Edinburgh, Edinburgh University Press, 1989), p. 241.

15. Jameson, 'Progress versus utopia', p. 150.

16. *ibid.*, p. 153.

17. Fredric Jameson, *The Political Unconscious* (London, Methuen, 1981), p. 42.

18. Teresa de Lauretis, 'Signs of w^a_onder', in Teresa de Lauretis, Andreas Huyssen, Kathleen Woodward (eds), *The Technological Imagination* (Madison, Coda Press, 1980), p. 170.

19. Fredric Jameson, 'Postmodernism and consumer society', in Hal Foster (ed.), *Postmodern Culture* (London, Pluto, 1985), p. 115.

20. Jean Baudrillard, 'Symbolic exchange and death', in Mark Poster (ed.), *Jean Baudrillard: Selected writings* (Cambridge, Polity Press/Basil Blackwell, 1988), p. 128.

21. Jean Baudrillard, 'Simulacra and science fiction', trans. Arthur B. Evans, *Science Fiction Studies*, 18, Part 3 (1991), p. 310.

22. Baudrillard, 'Symbolic exchange', p. 140.

23. *ibid.*, p. 145.

24. *ibid.*, p. 172.

25. Baudrillard, 'Simulacra', p. 311.

26. Jean Baudrillard, 'The year 2000 has already happened', in Arthur Kroker and Marilouise Kroker (eds), *Body Invaders: Sexuality and the postmodern condition* (London, Macmillan, 1988), p. 36.

27. S. Best and D. Kellner, *Postmodern Theory: Critical interrogations* (London, Macmillan, 1991), p. 142.

28. Baudrillard, 'Simulacra', pp. 311, 310 and 312.

29. *ibid.*, p. 311.

30. Fred Pfeil, *Another Tale to Tell: Politics and narrative in postmodern culture* (London, Verso, 1990), p. 88.

31. Huyssen, *After the Great Divide*, p. ix.

32. Linda Hutcheon, *The Politics of Postmodernism* (London, Methuen, 1989), p. 142.

33. Craig Owens, 'The discourse of others: Feminists and postmodernism', in Hal Foster (ed.), *Postmodern Culture* (London, Pluto, 1985), pp. 61–2.

34. *ibid.*, p. 61.

35. *ibid.*
36. Meaghan Morris, *The Pirate's Fiancée: Feminism, reading, post-modernism* (London and New York, Verso, 1988), p. 15.
37. *ibid.*, p. 16.
38. Christine Di Stefano, 'Dilemmas of difference: Feminism, modernity, and postmodernism', in Linda J. Nicholson (ed.), *Feminism/Postmodernism* (New York and London, Routledge, 1990), p. 75.
39. Sabina Lovibond, 'Feminism and postmodernism', in R. Boyne and A. Rattansi (eds), *Postmodernism and Society* (London, Macmillan, 1990), p. 172.
40. Sandra Harding, 'Feminism, science, and the anti-Enlightenment critique', in Nicholson (ed.), *Feminism/Postmodernism*, p. 99.
41. Nancy Fraser and Linda J. Nicholson, 'Social criticism without philosophy: An encounter between feminism and postmodernism', in Nicholson (ed.), *Feminism/Postmodernism*, p. 35.
42. Jean-François Lyotard, *The Postmodern Condition: A report on knowledge*, trans. G. Bennington and B. Massouri (Manchester, Manchester University Press, 1984), p. xxiii.
43. Jean-François Lyotard, 'Note on the meaning of the "post-"', in T. Docherty (ed.), *Postmodernism: A reader* (Hemel Hempstead, Harvester Wheatsheaf, 1993), pp. 48–9.
44. *op. cit.*, p. 23.
45. *ibid.*, p. 34.
46. Quoted in Toril Moi, *Sexual/Textual Politics* (London, Methuen, 1985), p. 12.
47. Toril Moi, 'Feminism, postmodernism, and style: recent feminist criticism in the United States', *Cultural Critique*, 9 (Spring, 1988), p. 7.
48. Laura Kipnis, 'Feminism: The political conscience of postmodernism?', in Ross (ed.), *Universal Abandon?*, p. 150. The phrase occurs in the context of a discussion of the relations between Marxism, feminist theory and psychoanalysis.
49. Anne Cranny-Francis, *Feminist Fiction: Feminist uses of generic fiction* (Cambridge, Polity Press/Basil Blackwell, 1990), p. 43.
50. Joanna Russ, *The Female Man* (New York, Bantam, 1975). Page references are to the 1985 edition (London, The Women's Press), here p. 212.
51. Mary C. Gentile, *Film Feminisms*, Westport, CT, Greenwood Press, 1985, p. 19. Gentile is here drawing on Kristeva's analysis of the female subject as a 'subject-in-the-making': see Elaine Marks and Isabelle de Courtivron (eds), *New French Feminisms* (Hemel Hempstead, Harvester Wheatsheaf, 1981), p. 167.
52. Joanna Russ, '*Amor vincit foeminam*: The battle of the sexes in science fiction', *Science Fiction Studies*, 7 (1980), pp. 8–9.
53. Pamela Sargent (ed.), *Women of Wonder: SF Stories by Women about*

Women (New York, Vintage, 1974; Harmondsworth, Penguin, 1978), p. 48.

54. Joanna Russ, 'The image of women in science fiction', in S.K. Cornillon (ed.), *Images of Women in Fiction: Feminist perspectives* (Bowling Green, OH, Bowling Green University Popular Press), p. 91.

55. Stuart Hall, 'Cultural identity and diaspora', in J. Rutherford (ed.), *Identity: Community, culture, difference* (London, Lawrence and Wishart, 1990), p. 225.

56. Takayuki Tatsumi, 'Some real mothers: An interview with Samuel R. Delany', in *Science Fiction Eye*, 1 (March 1988), p. 7.

57. Teresa de Lauretis, *Technologies of Gender: Essays on theory, film and fiction* (London, Macmillan, 1987), pp. 25 and ix.

58. Alice Jardine, *Gynesis: Configurations of women and modernity* (Ithaca and London, Cornell University Press, 1985), p. 25.

59. De Lauretis, *Technologies*, p. 2.

60. Julia Kristeva, 'Oscillation between power and denial', in Marks and de Courtivron (eds), *New French Feminisms*, p. 166.

61. Marleen Barr, *Feminist Fabulation: Space/postmodern fiction* (Iowa City, University of Iowa Press, 1992), p. 3.

62. *ibid.*, pp. 10 and 18.

63. Haraway, 'Manifesto for cyborgs', p. 71.

64. *ibid.*, pp. 99 and 100–1.

65. De Lauretis, *Technologies*, p. 10.

2 Unpredictable aliens

1. Jonathan Rutherford, 'A place called home: Identity and the cultural politics of difference', in Rutherford (ed.), *Identity*, p. 11.

2. Ursula Le Guin, *The Language of the Night: Essays on science fiction and fantasy* (London, The Women's Press, 1989), p. 85.

3. Quoted in Jeffrey Elliot, 'Future forum', *Future Life*, no. 17 (March 1980), p. 60.

4. Quoted in Ruth Salvaggio, 'Octavia Butler', in M. Barr, R. Salvaggio and R. Law, *Suzy McKee Charnas, Octavia Butler, Joan D. Vinge* (Washington, Starmont House, 1986), p. 7.

5. *ibid.*, p. 6.

6. Quoted in Sandra Y. Govan, 'Homage to tradition: Octavia Butler renovates the historical novel', *Melus*, 13, nos 1 and 2 (Spring–Summer 1986), p. 96.

7. Sandra Y. Govan, 'Connections, links, and extended networks: Patterns in Octavia Butler's science fiction', *Black American Literature Forum*, 18, no. 2 (Summer 1984), p. 84.

8. L. McCaffery, *Across the Wounded Galaxies* (Urbana and Chicago, University of Illinois Press, 1990), p. 64.

9. Octavia Butler, *Dawn* (London, Victor Gollancz, 1987). Page references are to the 1988 edition (London, VGSF); here p. 41.

10. Sondra O'Neale, 'Inhibiting midwives, usurping creators: The struggling emergence of black women in American fiction', in Teresa de Lauretis (ed.), *Feminist Studies/Critical Studies* (Bloomington, Indiana University Press, 1986), p. 153.

11. McCaffery, *Across the Wounded Galaxies*, p. 69.

12. Hoda Zaki, 'Utopia, dystopia, and ideology in the science fiction of Octavia Butler', *Science Fiction Studies*, 17, Part 2 (1990), p. 247.

13. McCaffery, *Across the Wounded Galaxies*, p. 68.

14. Octavia Butler, *Adulthood Rites* (London, Victor Gollancz, 1988). Page references are to the 1989 edition (London, VGSF); here p. 159.

15. Haraway, 'Manifesto for cyborgs', p. 72.

16. Haraway, 'Monkeys, aliens and women', p. 308.

17. Hall, 'Cultural identity and diaspora', p. 223.

18. Octavia Butler, *Mind of my Mind* (New York, Doubleday, 1977). Page references are to the 1978 edition (New York, Avon); here p. 55.

19. Pfeil, *Another Tale to Tell*, p. 93.

20. Haraway, 'Manifesto for cyborgs', p. 99.

21. Adele S. Newson, Review of *Dawn* and *Adulthood Rites*, *Black American Literature Forum*, 23, no. 2 (1989), p. 389.

22. Linda Hutcheon, 'Beginning to theorize postmodernism', *Textual Practice*, 1, Part 1 (1987), 10.

3 Destabilising gender and genre

1. Cranny-Francis, *Feminist Fiction*, p. 74.

2. Morris, *The Pirate's Fiancée*, p. 267.

3. Jane Flax, 'Postmodernism and gender relations in feminist theory', in *Signs: Journal of women in culture and society*, 12, no. 4 (1987), p. 623–4.

4. Fredric Jameson, 'Science fiction as a spatial genre: Generic discontinuities and the problem of figuration in Vonda McIntyre's *The Exile Waiting*', *Science Fiction Studies*, 14, Part 1 (1987), p. 58.

5. Anders Stephanson, 'Regarding postmodernism: A conversation with Fredric Jameson', *Social Text*, 6, no. 2 (1987), pp. 32–3.

6. *ibid.*, p. 43.

7. All the *Star Trek* books, including those written by Vonda McIntyre, also have a 'Centre', in this case 'Starbase' which represents the law of the father in the same way that the Centre does in McIntyre's other books.

8. Vonda McIntyre, *The Exile Waiting* (New York, Doubleday, 1975). Page references are to the 1985 edition (New York, Tor); here p. 43.

9. Vonda McIntyre, *Dreamsnake* (Houghton Mifflin, 1978; London, Gollancz, 1978). Page references are to the 1979 edition (London, Pan); here p. 195.

10. Vonda McIntyre, *Superluminal* (New York, Houghton Mifflin, 1983). Page references are to the 1984 edition (New York, Pocket); here p. 129.

11. Haraway, 'Manifesto for cyborgs', p. 97.

12. Vonda McIntyre, *The Entropy Effect* (New York, Pocket, 1981). Page references are to the 1988 edition (London, Titan); here p. 219.

13. Constance Penley gives a fascinating account of the way in which female fans of *Star Trek* write stories about the romantic, erotic relationship between Kirk and Spock, thus combining romance, pornography and utopian science fiction, and rethinking gender relations at the same time: see Constance Penley, 'Feminism, psychoanalysis, and the study of popular culture', in L. Grossberg *et al.* (eds), *Cultural Studies* (New York and London, Routledge, 1992), pp. 479–94.

14. C.J. Cherryh, *Forty Thousand in Gehenna* (West Bloomfield, MI, Phantasia Press, 1983). Page references are to the 1986 edition (London, Methuen); here p. 200.

15. C.J. Cherryh, *Cyteen* (New York, Warner, 1988). Page references are to the 1989 edition (New York, Popular Library); here p. 9.

16. Gwyneth Jones, 'Consider her ways . . .', *Foundation*, 48 (Spring 1990), p. 74.

4 Troubles in women's country

1. Suzy McKee Charnas, 'A woman appeared', in Marleen S. Barr (ed.), *Future Females: A critical anthology* (Bowling Green, OH, Bowling Green University Popular Press, 1981), p. 104.

2. *ibid.*, p. 106.

3. *ibid.*, p. 104.

4. Rita Felski, *Beyond Feminist Aesthetics* (London, Hutchinson Radius, 1989), p. 168.

5. Suzy McKee Charnas, *Walk to the End of the World* (New York, Ballantine, 1974). Page references are to the 1981 edition (London, Hodder and Stoughton); here p. 5.

6. Sarah Lefanu, *In the Chinks of the World Machine: Feminism and science fiction* (London, The Women's Press, 1988), p. 164.

7. Letter, 6 November 1980, quoted in Jeanne Gomoll, 'Out of context: Post-holocaust themes in feminist science fiction', *Janus*, Part 6 (Winter 1980), p. 15.

8. Sally Miller Gearhart, *The Wanderground* (Watertown, Ma., Perse-phone Press, 1979). Page references are to the 1985 edition (London, The Women's Press); here pp. 124–5.
9. James Tiptree, Jr, 'Houston, Houston, do you read?', in Vonda McIntrye and Susan Janice Anderson (eds), *Aurora: Beyond Equality* (New York, Fawcett, 1976) and in Tiptree, *Star Songs of an Old Primate* (anthology) (1978). Page references are to the 1978 edition (New York, Ballantine); here p. 220.
10. Felski, *Beyond Feminist Aesthetics*, p. 78.
11. Hutcheon, *Politics of Postmodernism*, p. 157.
12. Francis Bartkowski, *Feminist Utopias* (Lincoln and London, University of Nebraska Press, 1989), p. 161.
13. Søren Baggeson, 'Utopian and dystopian pessimism: Le Guin's *The Word for World is Forest* and Tiptree's "We who stole the dream"', in *Science Fiction Studies*, 14, Part 1 (1987), pp. 34–43.
14. Tom Moylan, *Demand the Impossible: Science fiction and the utopian imagination* (London, Methuen, 1986), p. 11.
15. *ibid.*, p. 51.
16. Constance Penley, 'Time travel, primal scene and the critical dystopia', in Annette Kuhn (ed.), *Alien Zone* (London and New York, Verso, 1990), p. 117.
17. Maria Minich Brewer, 'Surviving fictions: Gender and difference in postmodern and postnuclear narrative', *Discourse*, 9 (1987), p. 47.
18. Sheri Tepper, *The Gate to Women's Country* (New York, Doubleday, 1988). Page references are to the 1989 edition (London, Bantam); here p. 265.
19. Pamela Sargent, *The Shore of Women* (New York, Crown, 1986). Page references are to the 1987 edition (London, Chatto and Windus); here p. 95.
20. Margaret Atwood, *The Handmaid's Tale* (New York, Fawcett, 1986). Page references are to the 1987 edition (London, Virago Press); here p. 191.
21. Margaret Atwood in an interview with Claudia Dreyfus, *Progressive*, 56 (March 1992), pp. 32–3.
22. Mary McCarthy, review of *The Handmaid's Tale*, in *The New York Times Book Review*, 9 February 1986, p. 35.

5. Cyberpunk, cyborgs and feminist science fiction

1. See John Walker, 'Cyberpunk', in *Video Magazine*, 15 (January 1992), p. 78, for claims that cyberpunk has had an influence on interests as diverse as 'physical therapy pioneer Dr. Joseph M. Rosen' and 'the top brains at NASA's Ames Research Centre'.

2. Takayuki Tatsumi, 'Some real mothers: An interview with Samuel R. Delany' in *Science Fiction Eye*, 1 (March 1988), p. 9.
3. Joan Gordon, 'Yin and yang duke it out' in Larry McCaffery (ed.), *Storming the Reality Studio* (Durham and London, Duke University Press, 1991), p. 199.
4. Teresa de Lauretis, 'Signs of w$_a^o$nder', p. 167.
5. Istvan Csicsery-Ronay, 'Cyberpunk forum/symposium', in *Missippi Review*, 16, nos 2 and 3 (1988), p. 27. For further comment see also 'Cyberpunk and neuromanticism', pp. 266–78.
6. Larry McCaffery, 'The desert of the real: The cyberpunk controversy', *Missippi Review*, 16, nos 2 and 3 (1988), p. 9.
7. Gregory Benford, 'Is something going on?', *ibid.*, p. 22.
8. Bruce Sterling (ed.), *Mirrorshades* (London, Paladin, 1988), p. x.
9. Denny Atkin, 'The iceman cometh', *Omni*, 12 (August 1990), p. 82.
10. Tatsumi, *Science-Fiction Eye*, p. 9.
11. See Bruce Sterling's preface to William Gibson, *Burning Chrome* (London, Gollancz, 1986). Page references are to the 1988 edition (London, Grafton); here p. 9.
12. *ibid.*, p. 10.
13. Jameson, *Postmodernism, or, The Cultural Logic of Late Capitalism*, p. 386.
14. Lucius Shepard, 'Waiting for the barbarians', in *Journal Wired*, Part 1 (Winter 1989), p. 115.
15. Sterling, *Mirrorshades*, p. xiii.
16. Sterling, Preface to Gibson's *Burning Chrome*, p. 12.
17. McCaffery, *Across the Wounded Galaxies*, p. 135.
18. Veronica Hollinger, 'Cybernetic deconstructions: Cyberpunk and postmodernism', in L. McCaffery, *Storming the Reality Studio*, p. 212.
19. Csicsery-Ronay, *op. cit.*, p. 271.
20. Pam Rosenthal, 'Jacked-in: Fordism, cyberpunk, Marxism', *Socialist Review* (Spring 1991), p. 89.
21. Jameson, *op. cit.*, p. 286.
22. Sterling, *Mirrorshades*, p. ix.
23. Shepard, 'Waiting for the barbarians', p. 108.
24. Andrew Ross, *Strange Weather: Culture, science and technology* (London, Verso, 1991), p. 153.
25. Hollinger, in *Storming the Reality Studio*, p. 204.
26. Ross, *Strange Weather*, p. 145.
27. Timothy Leary, 'The cyberpunk: The individual as reality pilot', *Missippi Review*, 16, nos 2 and 3, p. 253.
28. Janet Wolff, *Feminine Sentences* (Cambridge, Polity Press/Basil Blackwell, 1990), see particularly pp. 34–50.
29. William Gibson, *Neuromancer* (London, Gollancz, 1984). Page references are to the 1986 edition (London, Grafton); here p. 57.

30. *ibid.*, p. 60.
31. William Gibson, *Mona Lisa Overdrive* (London, Gollancz, 1988). Page references are to the 1989 edition (London, Grafton); here p. 101.
32. Gibson, *Neuromancer*, p. 14.
33. Gibson made this remark in an interview with Victoria Hamburg, 'The king of cyberpunk', *Interview*, 19 (January 1989), p. 84.
34. William Gibson, *Count Zero* (London, Gollancz, 1986). Page references are to the 1987 edition (London, Grafton); here pp. 278–9.
35. Gibson, *Mona Lisa Overdrive*, pp. 168–9.
36. Vivian Sobchak, 'Cities on the edge of time', *East–West Film Journal*, 3, Part 1 (1988), p. 14.
37. Jameson, *Postmodernism, or, the Cultural Logic of Late Capitalism*, p. 33.
38. Ross, *Strange Weather*, p. 155.
39. Gibson, *Burning Chrome*, p. 141.
40. Peter Sloterdijk, 'Cynicism: The twilight of false consciousness' *New German Critique*, 33 (1984), p. 192.
41. Claudia Springer, 'The pleasure of the interface', *Screen*, 32, no. 3 (1991), p. 306.
42. McCaffery, *Across the Wounded Galaxies*, p. 139.
43. Springer, 'The pleasure of the interface', pp. 307–8.
44. Sterling, *Mirrorshades*, p. xi.
45. Delany, *Missippi Review*, nos 2 and 3, p. 33.
46. Constance Penley and Andrew Ross, 'Cyborgs at large: Interview with Donna Haraway', *Social Text*, 25/6 (1990), p. 20.
47. S. Bukatman, 'Postcards from the posthuman solar system', *Science Fiction Studies*, 18, Part 3 (1991), p. 351.
48. Pat Cadigan, *Patterns* (New York, Ursus Imprints, 1989). Page references are to the 1991 edition (London, Grafton); here pp. 202–3.
49. Sterling, *Mirrorshades*, p. xii.
50. Judith Butler, *Gender Trouble* (New York and London, Routledge, 1990), p. 9.
51. Haraway, 'Manifesto for cyborgs', p. 72.
52. Bill Nichols, 'The work of culture in the age of cybernetic systems', *Screen*, 29, no. 1 (1988), p. 44.
53. Rebecca Ore, *The Illegal Rebirth of Billy the Kid* (New York, Tor, 1991), p. 56.
54. Marge Piercy, *Body of Glass* (London, Michael Joseph, 1992), p. 73.
55. George Slusser, 'Literary MTV', in McCaffery (ed.), *Storming the Reality Studio*, p. 340.
56. Sterling, *op. cit.*, p. xiii.
57. Csicsery-Ronay, *op. cit.*, p. 267.

Bibliography

Aldiss, B. with D. Wingrove (1986) *Trillion Year Spree*, London, Gollancz.

Adam, I., and H. Tiffin (eds) (1991) *Past the Last Post: Theorizing post-colonialism and post-modernism*, Hemel Hempstead, Harvester Wheatsheaf.

Appignanesi, L. (ed.) (1986) *Postmodernism. ICA Documents 4*, London, Institute of Contemporary Arts.

Arac, J. (ed.) (1986) *Postmodernism and Politics*, Manchester, Manchester University Press.

Arac, J. (1987) *Critical Genealogies: Historical situations for postmodern literary studies*, New York, Columbia University Press.

Armit, L. (ed.) (1991) *Where No Man has Gone Before: Women and Science Fiction*, London and New York, Routledge.

Atkin, D. (1990) 'The iceman cometh', *Omni*, 12 (August), 82.

Atwood, M. (1987) *The Handmaid's Tale*, London, Virago.

Baggeson, S. (1987) 'Utopian and dystopian pessimism: Le Guin's *The Word for World is Forest* and Tiptree's "We who stole the dream"', *Science Fiction Studies*, 14, Part 1, 34–43.

Balsamo, A. (1987) 'Unwrapping the postmodern: A feminist glance', *Journal Of Communication Inquiry*, 11, 64–72.

Balsamo, A. (1988) 'Reading cyborgs writing feminism', *Communication*, 10, 334–44.

Barr, M.S. (ed.) (1981) *Future Females: A critical anthology*, Bowling Green, OH, Bowling Green University Popular Press.

Barr, M.S. (1987) *Alien To Femininity: Speculative fiction and feminist theory*, Westport CT, Greenwood Press.

Barr, M.S. (1992) *Feminist Fabulation: Space/postmodern fiction*, Iowa City, University of Iowa Press.

Bartkowski, F. (1989) *Feminist Utopias*, Lincoln and London, University of Nebraska Press.

Baudrillard, J. (1973) *The Mirror of Production*, trans. Mark Poster (1975) St Louis, Telos Press.

Baudrillard, J. (1976) *For a Critique of the Political Economy of the Sign*, trans. Charles Levin (1981), St Louis, Telos Press.

Baudrillard, J. (1977) *Forget Foucault*, trans. Nicole Dufresne (1987), New York, Semiotext(e).

Baudrillard, J. (1979) *Seduction*, trans. Brian Singer (1990), London, Macmillan.

Baudrillard, J. (1981) *Simulations*, trans. Paul Foss, Paul Patton and Philip Beitchman (1983), New York, Semiotext(e).

Baudrillard, J. (1983a) *In the Shadow of the Silent Majorities*, trans. Paul Foss, Paul Patton and John Johnston (1983), New York, Semiotext(e).

Baudrillard, J. (1983b) *Fatal Strategies*, trans. Philip Beitchman and W.G.J. Nieluchowski, ed. Jim Flemming (1990), New York, Semiotext(e); London, Pluto.

Baudrillard, J. (1986) *America*, trans. Chris Turner (1988), London and New York, Verso.

Baudrillard, J. (1987) *Cool Memories*, trans. Chris Turner (1990), London and New York, Verso.

Baudrillard, J. (1988) *Selected Writings*, ed. Mark Poster, Cambridge, Polity Press/Basil Blackwell.

Baudrillard, J. (1991a) Simulacra and science fiction', trans. Arthur B. Evans, *Science Fiction Studies*, 18, Part 3, 309–13.

Baudrillard, J. (1991b) Ballard's *Crash*, trans. Arthur B. Evans, *Science Fiction Studies*, 18, Part 3, 313–20.

Bauman, Z. (1987) *Legislators and Interpreters: On modernity, post-modernity and intellectuals*, Ithaca, Cornell University Press.

Bell, D. (1973) *The Coming of Post-Industrial Society*, New York, Basic Books.

Bell, D. (1976) *The Cultural Contradictions of Capitalism*, New York, Basic Books.

Belsey, C. (1980) *Critical Practice*, London, Methuen.

Benford, G. (1988) 'Is something going on?' *Missippi Review*, 16, nos 2 and 3, 18–23.

Benhabib, S. (1984) 'Epistomologies of postmodernism: A rejoinder to Jean-François Lyotard', *New German Critique*, 33, 103–26.

Bennington, G. (1988) *Lyotard: Writing the event*, Manchester, Manchester University Press.

Berman, R.A. (1987) 'The routinization of charismatic modernism and the problem of postmodernity', *Cultural Critique*, 5, 49–68.

Bernstein, R.J. (ed.) (1985) *Habermas and Modernity*, Cambridge, Polity Press/Basil Blackwell.

Bertens, H. (1983) 'The postmodern *Weltanschaung* and its relation with modernism: an introductory survey', in D. Fokkema and H. Bertens (eds)

(1986) *Approaching Postmodernism*, Amsterdam and Philadelphia, John Benjamins, 9–51.

Best, S., and D. Kellner (1991) *Postmodern Theory: Critical interrogations*, London, Macmillan.

Bonner, F. (1990) 'Difference and desire, slavery and seduction: Octavia Butler's *Xenogenesis*', *Foundation*, 48, 50–62.

Boyne, R., and A. Rattansi (eds) (1990) *Postmodernism and Society*, London, Macmillan.

Braidotti, R., (1991) *Patterns of Dissonance: Study of women and contemporary philosophy*, Cambridge, Polity Press/Basil Blackwell.

Brewer, M.M. (1987) 'Surviving fictions: Gender and difference in postmodern and postnuclear narrative', *Discourse*, 9, 37–52.

Brooker, P. (1992) *Modernism/Postmodernism*, London and New York, Longman.

Bukatman, S. (1989) 'The cybernetic (city) state: Terminal space becomes phenomenal', *Journal of the Fantastic in the Arts*, 2 (Summer), 43–63.

Bukatman, S. (1991) 'Postcards from the posthuman solar system', *Science Fiction Studies*, 18, Part 3, 343–57.

Burger, P. (1974) *Theory of the Avant-Garde*, trans. M. Shaw, Manchester, Manchester University Press.

Butler, J. (1990) *Gender Trouble*, New York and London, Routledge.

Butler, O. (1976) *Patternmaster*, New York, Doubleday.

Butler, O. (1978) *Mind of my Mind*, New York, Avon.

Butler, O. (1979) *Kindred*, New York, Doubleday.

Butler, O. (1980) *Wild Seed*, London, Sidgwick and Jackson.

Butler, O. (1985) *Clay's Ark*, London, Arrow.

Butler, O. (1987) *Dawn*, London, VGSF.

Butler, O. (1988) *Adulthood Rites*, London, VGSF.

Butler, O. (1989) *Imago*, London, VGSF.

Cadigan, P. (1987) *Mindplayers*, New York, Bantam Spectra.

Cadigan, P. (1991a) *Patterns*, London, Grafton.

Cadigan, P. (1991b) *Synners*, New York, Bantam.

Calinescu, M., (1987) *Five Faces of Modernity: Modernism, avant-garde, decadence, kitsch, postmodernism*, Durham, NC, Duke University Press.

Calinescu, M., and D. Fokkema (eds) (1988) *Exploring Postmodernism*, Amsterdam and Philadelphia, John Benjamins.

Callinicos, A., (1989) *Against Postmodernism*, Cambridge, Polity Press/ Basil Blackwell.

Carr, H. (ed.) (1989) *From my Guy to Sci-Fi: Genre and women's writing in the postmodern world*, London, Pandora Press.

Carter, P.A. (1977) *The Creation of Tomorrow: Fifty years of magazine science fiction*, New York, Columbia University Press.

Chambers, I. (1990) *Border Dialogues: Journeys in postmodernity*, London and New York, Comedia/Routledge.

Charnas, S. McKee (1980) *Motherlines*, London, Gollancz.

Charnas, S. McKee (1981a) 'A woman appeared' in M. Barr (ed.) *Future Females*, Bowling Green, OH, Bowling Green University Press.

Charnas, S. McKee (1981b) *Walk To the End of the World*, London, Hodder and Stoughton.

Cherryh, C.J. (1983) *The Pride of Chanur*, London, Methuen.

Cherryh, C.J. (1984) *Chanur's Venture*, New York, Daw.

Cherryh, C.J. (1985) *The Kif Strike Back*, New York, Daw.

Cherryh, C.J. (1986a) *Forty Thousand in Gehenna*, London, Methuen.

Cherryh, C.J. (1986b) *Chanur's Homecoming*, New York, Daw.

Cherryh, C.J. (1989a) *Cyteen: The betrayal*, New York, Popular Library.

Cherryh, C.J. (1989b) *Cyteen: The rebirth*, New York, Popular Library.

Cherryh, C.J. (1989c) *Cyteen: The vindication*, New York, Popular Library.

Cixous, H. (1981) 'The laugh of the Medusa', in E. Marks and I. de Courtivron (eds) *New French Feminisms*, Hemel Hempstead, Harvester Wheatsheaf.

Collins, J. (1989) *Uncommon Cultures*, New York and London, Routledge.

Cook, D. and A. Kroker (1988) *The Postmodern Scene, Excremental Culture and Hyper-Aesthetics*, London, Macmillan.

Connor, S. (1990) *Postmodernist Culture: An introduction to theories of the contemporary*, Oxford, Basil Blackwell.

Cournillon, S.K. (ed.) (1972) *Images of Women in Fiction: Feminist perspectives*, Bowling Green, OH, Bowling Green University Popular Press.

Coward, R. (1984) *Female Desire*, London, Paladin.

Cranny-Francis, A. (1990) *Feminist Fiction: Feminist uses of generic fiction*, Cambridge, Polity Press/Basil Blackwell.

Creed, B. (1987) 'From here to modernity: Feminism and postmodernism', *Screen*, 28 Part 2, 47–67.

Creed, B. (1986) 'Horror and the monstrous feminine: An imaginary abjection', *Screen*, 27, Part 1, 44–70.

Csicsery-Ronay, I. (1988) 'Cyberpunk and neuromanticism', *Missippi Review*, 16, nos 2 and 3, 266–78.

Csicsery-Ronay, I. (1991) 'The SF of theory: Baudrillard and Haraway', *Science Fiction Studies*, 18, Part 3, 387–403.

Delany, S. (1987) 'The semiology of silence', *Science Fiction Studies*, 14, Part 2, 134–64.

Delany, S. (1988) 'Is cyberpunk a good thing or a bad thing?', *Missippi Review*, 16, nos 2 and 3, 28–35.

de Lauretis, T. (1980) 'Signs of W$_{o}^{a}$nder' in T. de Lauretis, A. Huyssen, K. Woodward (eds) *The Technological Imagination*, Madison, Coda Press, 159–74.

de Lauretis, T. (ed.) (1986) *Feminist Studies/Critical Studies*, Bloomington, Indiana University Press.

de Lauretis, T. (1987) *Technologies of Gender: Essays on theory, film, and fiction*, London, Macmillan.

Denzin, N.K. (1991) *Images of Postmodern Society*, London, Sage.

Di Stefano, C. (1990) 'Dilemmas of difference: Feminism, modernity, and postmodernism', in L.J. Nicholson (ed.) *Feminism/Postmodernism*, New York and London, Routledge, 63–82.

Docherty, T. (ed.) (1993) *Postmodernism: A reader*, Hemel Hempstead, Harvester Wheatsheaf.

Donald, J. (ed.) (1991) *Psychoanalysis and Cultural Theory*, London, Macmillan.

Dreyfuss, C. (1992) 'Margaret Atwood: "Respectability can kill you very quickly"', *Progressive*, 56 (March), 30–3.

Eagleton, T. (1985) 'Capitalism, modernism and postmodernism', *New Left Review*, 152, 60–73. Reprinted in T. Eagleton, *Against the Grain*.

Eagleton, T. (1986) *Against the Grain: Essays 1975–1985*, London, Verso.

Easterbrook, N. (1992) 'The arc of our destruction: Reversal and erasure in cyberpunk', *Science Fiction Studies*, 19, Part 3, 378–94.

Ebert, T. (1980) 'The convergence of postmodern innovative fiction and science fiction', *Poetics Today*, 1, Part 4, 91–104.

Ecker, G. (ed.) (1985) *Feminist Aesthetics*, London, The Women's Press.

Eco, U. (1987) *Travels in Hyperreality*, trans. W. Weaver, London, Picador.

Elliot, J. (1980) 'Future forum', *Future Life*, 17 (March), 59–62.

Featherstone, M. (1990) *Consumer Culture and Postmodernism*, London, Sage.

Fekete, J. (ed.) (1988) *Life after Postmodernism: Essays on value and culture*, London, Macmillan.

Felski, R. (1989) *Beyond Feminist Aesthetics*, London, Hutchinson Radius.

Ferguson, R., M. Gever, T. T. Minh-ha, C. West (eds) (1990) *Out There: Marginalisation and contemporary cultures*, Cambridge, MA, The New Museum of Contemporary Art/MIT Press.

Ferguson, R., W. Olander, M. Tucker, K. Fiss (eds) (1990) *Discourses: Conversations in postmodern art and culture*, New York, The New Museum of Contemporary Art/MIT Press.

Fiedler, L.A. (1975) 'Cross the border – close that gap: postmodernism', in M. Cunliffe (ed.) *American Literature Since 1900*, London, Sphere Books, 344–66.

Flax, J. (1987) 'Postmodernism and gender relations in feminist theory', *Signs*, 12, no. 4, 621–43. Reprinted in L. Nicholson (ed.), *Feminism/Postmodernism*, New York and London, Routledge, 39–62.

Flax, J. (1990) *Thinking Fragments: Psychoanalysis, feminism, and postmodernism in the contemporary west*, Berkley, Los Angeles, Oxford, University of California Press.

Fokkema, D., and H. Bertens (eds) (1986) *Approaching Postmodernism*, Amsterdam and Philadelphia, John Benjamins.

Foster, F.S. (1982) 'Octavia Butler's black female future fiction', *Extrapolation*, 23, no. 1, 37–48.

Foster, H. (ed.) (1985) *Postmodern Culture*, London and Sydney, Pluto Press. First published as (1983) *The Anti-Aesthetic: Essays on postmodern culture*, Port Townsend, Bay Press.

Foster, H. (1985) *Recodings: Art, spectacle, cultural politics*, Port Townsend, Bay Press.

Franklin, S., C. Lury and J. Stacey (eds) (1991) *Off-Centre: Feminism and cultural studies*, London, HarperCollins Academic.

Frankovits, A. (ed.) (1984) *Seduced and Abandoned: The Baudrillard scene*, New York, Semiotext(e).

Fraser, N. (1985) 'What's critical about critical theory? The case of Habermas and gender', *New German Critique*, 35, 97–131.

Fraser, N., and L. Nicholson (1988) 'Social criticism without philosophy: An encounter between feminism and postmodernism', *Theory, Culture and Society*, 5, nos. 2 and 3, 373–94. Reprinted in L. Nicholson (ed.) (1990) *Feminism/Postmodernism*, New York and London, Routledge, 19–38.

Friend, B. (1982) 'Time travel as a feminist didactic in works by Phyllis Eisenstein, Marlys Millhiser, and Octavia Butler', *Extrapolation*, 23, no. 1. 50–5.

Gane, M. (1991) *Baudrillard's Bestiary; Baudrillard and Culture*, London, Routledge.

Garnett, R. and R. J. Ellis (eds) (1989) *Science Fiction Roots and Branches: Contemporary critical approaches*, London, Macmillan.

Gearhart, S. M. (1985) *The Wanderground*, London, The Women's Press.

Gentile, M. (1985) *Film Feminisms*, Westport, CT, Greenwood Press.

Gibson, W. (1986) *Neuromancer*, London, Grafton.

Gibson, W. (1987) *Count Zero*, London, Grafton.

Gibson, W. (1988) *Burning Chrome*, London, Grafton.

Gibson, W. (1989) *Mona Lisa Overdrive*, London, Grafton.

Giddens A. (1981) 'Modernism and postmodernism', *New German Critique*, 22, 15–18.

Glass, F. (1989) 'The "New Bad Future": *Robocop* and 1980s Sci-Fi films', *Science as Culture*, no. 5, 6–49.

Gomoll, J. (1980) 'Out of context: post-holocaust themes in feminist science fiction', *Janus*, Part 6 (Winter), 14–17.

Gordon, J. (1990) 'Yin and yang duke it out: is cyberpunk feminism's new age?', *Science Fiction Eye*, 2, 37–40. Reprinted in L. McCaffery (ed.) *Storming the Reality Studio*, Durham and London, Duke University Press, 196–202.

Govan, S. Y. (1984) 'Connections, links, and extended networks: Patterns in Octavia Butler's science fiction', *Black American Literature Forum*, 18, no. 2, 82–7.

Govan, S. Y. (1986) 'Homage to tradition: Octavia Butler renovates the historical novel', *Melus*, 13, nos 1 and 2, 79–96.

Grant, G. (1990) 'Transcendence through detournement in William Gibson's *Neuromancer*', *Science Fiction Studies*, 17, Part 1, 41–9.

Green, J., and S. Lefanu (eds) (1985) *Dispatches from the Frontiers of the Female Mind*, London, The Women's Press.

Greene, G. and C. Kahn (eds) (1985) *Making a Difference: Feminist literary criticism*, London, Methuen.

Grossberg L., C. Nelson, P. Treichler (eds) (1992) *Cultural Studies*, New York and London, Routledge.

Hacker, M. (1977) 'Science fiction and feminism: The work of Joanna Russ', *Chrysalis*, no. 4, 69–79.

Hall, S. (1990) 'Cultural identity and diaspora', in J. Rutherford, (ed.) *Identity: Community, culture, difference*, London, Lawrence and Wishart, 222–37.

Hamburg, V. (1989) 'The king of cyberpunk', *Interview*, 19, (January), 84–6, 91.

Haraway, D. (1985) 'A manifesto for cyborgs: Science, technology, and socialist feminism in the 1980s', *Socialist Review*, Part 80, 65–107.

Haraway, D. (1989a) 'Monkeys, aliens, and women: love, science, and politics at the intersection of feminist theory and colonial discourse', *Women's Studies International Forum*, 12, no. 3, 295–312.

Haraway, D. (1989b) *Primate Visions: Gender, race, and nature in the world of modern science*, New York and London, Routledge.

Haraway, D. (1991) *Simians, Cyborgs and Women*, London, Free Association.

Haraway, D. (1992) 'The promises of monsters: A regenerative politics for inappropriate/d others', in Lawrence Grossberg, Cary Nelson, Paula Treichler (eds), *Cultural Studies*, New York and London, Routledge, 295–337.

Harding, S. (1986) 'The instability of the analytical categories of feminist theory', *Signs*, 11, no. 4, 645–64.

Harding, S. (1990) 'Feminism, science, and the anti-Enlightenment critique', in L. Nicholson (ed.) *Feminism/Postmodernism*, New York and London, Routledge, 83–106.

Harvey, D. (1989) *The Condition of Postmodernity*, Oxford, Basil Blackwell.

Hassan, I. (1987) *The Postmodern Turn: Essays in postmodern theory and culture*, Columbus, Ohio State University Press.

Hassan, I., and S. Hassan (eds) (1983) *Innovation/Renovation: New perspectives on the humanities*, Madison, University of Wisconsin Press.

Hebdige, D. (1987) 'The impossible object: Towards a sociology of the sublime', *New Formations*, no. 1, 47–76.

Hebdige, D. (1988) *Hiding in the Light: On images and things*, London and New York, Routledge/Comedia.

Hollinger, V. (1989) 'The vampire and the alien: Variations on the outsider', *Science Fiction Studies*, 16, Part 2, 145–59.

Hollinger, V. (1990a) 'Cybernetic deconstructions: cyberpunk and postmodernism', *Mosaic*, 23, Part 2, 29–44. Reprinted in L. McCaffery (ed.) (1991) *Storming the Reality Studio*, Durham and London, Duke University Press, 203–18.

Hollinger, V. (1990b) 'Feminist science fiction', *Extrapolation*, 31, no. 3, 229–39.

Hutcheon, L. (1987a) 'Beginning to theorize postmodernism', *Textual Practice*, 1, Part 1, 10–31.

Hutcheon, L. (1987b) 'The politics of postmodernism: Parody and history', *Cultural Critique*, 5, 179–207.

Hutcheon, L. (1988) *A Poetics of Postmodernism: History, theory, fiction*, London, Routledge.

Hutcheon, L. (1989) *The Politics of Postmodernism*, London, Methuen.

Huyssen, A. (1986) *After the Great Divide: Modernism, mass culture, postmodernism*, Bloomington, Indiana University Press.

Irigaray, L. (1981) 'This sex which is not one', in E. Marks and I. de Courtivron (eds) *New French Feminisms*, Hemel Hempstead, Harvester Wheatsheaf, 99–106.

Jameson, F. (1981) *The Political Unconscious*, London, Methuen.

Jameson, F. (1982) 'Progress versus utopia; or, can we imagine the future?', *Science Fiction Studies*, 9, Part 2, 147–58.

Jameson, F. (1984) 'The politics of theory: Ideological positions in the postmodern debate', *New German Critique*, 33, 53–65.

Jameson, F. (1985) 'Postmodernism and consumer society', in Hal Foster (ed.) *Postmodern Culture*, London, Pluto Press, 111–25. Also published in E. A. Kaplan (ed.) (1988) *Postmodernism and its Discontents*, London, Verso, 13–29.

Jameson, F. (1987) 'Science fiction as a spatial genre: Generic discontinuities and the problem of figuration in Vonda McIntyre's *The Exile Waiting*', *Science Fiction Studies*, 14, Part 1, 44–59.

Jameson, F. (1988) *The Ideologies of Theory*, 2 vols, London, Routledge.

Jameson, F. (1991a) *Postmodernism, or, The Cultural Logic of Late Capitalism*, London and New York, Verso.

Jameson, F. (1991b) *Signatures of the Visible*, London, Routledge.

Jardine, A. (1985) *Gynesis: Configurations of women and modernity*, Ithaca and London, Cornell University Press.

Jencks, C. (1986) *What is Postmodernism?*, London, Academy Editions.

Jencks, C. (1987) *Postmodernism*, London, Academy Editions.

Jones, G. (1984) *Divine Endurance*, London, Allen and Unwin.

Jones, G. (1986) *Escape Plans*, London, Unwin Paperbacks.

Jones, G. (1990) 'Consider Her Ways . . .', *Foundation*, 48, 70–9.

Jones, G. (1992) *White Queen*, London, VGSF.

Kadrey, R., (1989) 'Cyberpunk 101 reading list', *Whole Earth Review*, Summer, 83.

Kaplan, C. (1986) *Sea Changes: Essays on culture and feminism*, London, Verso.

Kaplan, E. A. (ed.) (1988) *Postmodernism and its Discontents*, London, Verso.

Kaveney, R. (1989) 'The science fictiveness of women's science fiction', in H. Carr (ed.) *From my Guy to Sci-Fi*, London, Pandora Press, 78–97.

Kellner, D. (1988) *Jean Baudrillard, from Marxism to Postmodernism and Beyond*, Cambridge, Polity Press/Basil Blackwell.

Kellner, D. (ed.) (1990) *Postmodernism/Jameson/Critique*, Washington, Maisonneuve Press.

Ketterer, D. (1989) 'Margaret Atwood's *The Handmaid's Tale*: A contextual dystopia', *Science Fiction Studies*, 16, Part 2, 209–17.

Kipnis, L. (1989) 'Feminism: The political conscience of postmodernism?', in A. Ross (ed.) *Universal Abandon? The politics of postmodernism*, Edinburgh, Edinburgh University Press, 149–66.

Kristeva, J. (1981) 'Oscillation between power and denial', in E. Marks and I. de Courtivron (eds) *New French Feminisms*, Brighton, Harvester, 137–41.

Kroker, A and M. Kroker (eds) (1988) *Body Invaders: Sexuality and the postmodern condition*, London, Macmillan.

Kuhn, A. (1982) *Women's Pictures*, London, Routledge and Kegan Paul.

Kuhn, A. (ed.) (1990) *Alien Zone*, London, Verso.

Lash, S. (1990) *Sociology of Postmodernism*, London, Routledge.

Leary, T. (1988) 'The cyber-punk: The individual as reality pilot', *Missippi Review*, 16, nos. 2 and 3, 252–65.

Le Doeuff, M. (1990) *Women and Philosophy*, Oxford, Basil Blackwell.

Lefanu, S. (1988) *In the Chinks of the World Machine: Feminism and science fiction*, London, The Women's Press.

Lefanu, S. (1989) 'Popular writing and feminist intervention in science fiction', in D. Longhurst (ed.) *Gender, Genre and Narrative Pleasure*, London, Unwin Hyman, 177–91.

Le Guin, U. (1989) *The Language of the Night: Essays on science fiction and fantasy*, London, The Women's Press.

Longhurst, D. (ed.) (1989) *Gender, Genre and Narrative Pleasure*, London, Unwin Hyman.

Lovibond, S. (1990) 'Feminism and postmodernism', in R. Boyne and A. Rattansi (eds) *Postmodernism and Society*, London, Macmillan, 154–86.

Luckhurst, R. (1991) 'Border policing: Postmodernism and science fiction', *Science Fiction Studies*, 18, Part 3, 358–66.

Lyotard, J.-F. (1983) 'Answering the question: What is postmodernism?', in I. Hassan and S. Hassan (eds) *Innovation/Renovation*, Madison, University of Wisconsin Press, 71–82.

Lyotard, J.-F. (1984) *The Postmodern Condition: A report on knowledge*, trans. G. Bennington and B. Massouri, Manchester, Manchester University Press.

Lyotard, J.-F. (1992) *The Postmodern Explained to Children*, London, Turnaround.

Marks E. and I. de Courtivron (eds) (1981) *New French Feminisms*, Brighton, Harvester.

McCabe, C. (ed.) (1986) *High Theory/Low Culture*, Manchester, University of Manchester Press.

McCaffery, L. (ed.) (1986) *Postmodern Fiction: A bio-bibliography*, Westport, CT, Greenwood Press.

McCaffery, L. (1988) 'The desert of the real: The cyberpunk controversy', *Missippi Review*, 16, nos 2 and 3, 7–15.

McCaffery, L. (1990) *Across the Wounded Galaxies*, Urbana and Chicago, University of Illinois Press.

McCaffery, L. (ed.) (1991) *Storming the Reality Studio*, Durham, NC, Duke University Press.

McCarthy, M. (1986) 'Breeders, wives and unwomen', *New York Times Book Review*, 9 February.

McHale, B. (1987) *Postmodernist Fiction*, London and New York, Methuen.

McHale, B. (1991) 'PostcyberMODERNpunkISM', in L. McCaffery (ed.) *Storming the Reality Studio*, Durham and London, Duke University Press, 308–23.

McIntyre, V. (1979) *Dreamsnake*, London, Pan.

McIntyre, V. (1984) *Superluminal*, New York, Pocket.

McIntyre, V. (1985) *The Exile Waiting*, New York, Tor.

McIntyre, V. (1988) *The Entropy Effect*, London, Titan.

McIntyre, V. (1989) *Starfarers*, New York, Ace.

McIntyre, V. (1990) *Transition*, New York, Bantam.

McIntyre, V. (1992) *Metaphase*, New York, Bantam.

McIntyre, V. and S. J. Anderson (eds) (1976) *Aurora: Beyond equality*, New York, Fawcett.

McRobbie, A. (1986) 'Postmodernism and popular culture', in L. Appignanesi (ed.) *Postmodernism: ICA documents 4*, London, ICA, 54–8.

Minh-ha, T.T. (1989) *Woman, Native, Other*, Bloomington, Indiana University Press.

Modleski, T. (ed.) (1986) *Studies in Entertainment*, Bloomington, Indiana University Press.

Modleski, T. (1991) *Feminism without Women*, New York and London, Routledge.

Moi, T. (1985) *Sexual/Textual Politics*, London, Methuen.

Moi, T. (ed.) (1986) *The Kristeva Reader*, Oxford, Basil Blackwell.

Moi, T. (1988) 'Feminism, postmodernism, and style: Recent feminist criticism in the United States', *Cultural Critique*, 9 (Spring), 3–22.

Monk. P. (1980) 'Frankenstein's daughters: The problem of the feminine image in science fiction', *Mosaic*, 13, Parts 3–4, 15–27.

Morris, M. (1988) *The Pirate's Fiancée: Feminism, reading, postmodernism*, London and New York, Verso.

Mouffe, C. (1989) 'Radical democracy: Modern or postmodern?', in A. Ross (ed.) *Universal Abandon? The politics of postmodernism*, Edinburgh, Edinburgh University Press, 31–45.

Moylan, T. (1986) *Demand the Impossible: Science fiction and the utopian imagination*, London, Methuen.

Nelson, C., and L. Grossberg (eds) (1988) *Marxism and the Interpretation of Culture*, London, Macmillan.

Newson, A. (1989) Review of Octavia Butler's *Dawn* and *Adulthood Rites*, *Black American Literature Forum*, 23, no. 2, 389–96.

Nichols, B. (1988) 'The work of culture in the age of cybernetic systems', *Screen*, 29, no. 1, 22–46.

Nicholson, L. (ed.) (1990) *Feminism/Postmodernism*, New York and London, Routledge.

Nixon, N. (1992) 'Cyberpunk: Preparing the ground for revolution or keeping the boys satisfied?', *Science Fiction Studies*, 19, Part 3, 219–35.

Norris, C. (1990) *What's Wrong with Postmodernism: Critical theory and the ends of philosophy*, Hemel Hempstead, Harvester Wheatsheaf.

O'Neale, S. (1986) 'Inhibiting midwives, usurping creators: The struggling emergence of black women in American fiction', in T. de Lauretis (ed.) *Feminist Studies/Critical Studies*, Bloomington, Indiana University Press, 139–56.

Ore, R. (1988) *Becoming Alien*, New York, Tor.

Ore, R. (1989) *Being Alien*, New York, Tor.

Ore, R. (1990) *Human to Human*, New York, Tor.

Ore, R. (1991) *The Illegal Rebirth of Billy the Kid*, New York, Tor.

Owens, C. (1985) 'The discourse of others: Feminists and postmodernism', in Hal Foster (ed.) *Postmodern Culture*, London and Sydney, Pluto Press, 57–82.

Parrinder, P. (1976) 'The alien encounter: Or, Ms Brown and Mrs Le Guin', *Science Fiction Studies*, 3, Part 1. Reprinted in P. Parrinder (ed.) (1979) *SF: A critical guide*, London, Longman, 148–61.

Parrinder, P. (1980) *Science Fiction: Its criticism and teaching*, London, Methuen.

Paulsen, I.-L. (1984) 'Can women fly?: Vonda McIntyre's *Dreamsnake* and Sally Gearhart's *The Wanderground*', *Women's Studies International Forum*, 7, no. 2, 103–10.

Pawling, C. (ed.) (1984) *Popular Fiction and Social Change*, London, Macmillan.

Penley, C. (1990) 'Time travel, primal scene and the critical dystopia' in A. Kuhn (ed.) *Alien Zone*, London and New York, Verso, 116–27.

Penley, C. (1992) 'Feminism, psychoanalysis, and the study of the popular', in L. Grossberg, C. Nelson and P. Treichler (eds) *Cultural Studies*, New York and London, Routledge, 479–94.

Penley, C. and A. Ross (1990) 'Cyborgs at large: Interview with Donna Haraway', *Social Text*, Part 25/6, 8–23.

Perloff, M. (1986) *The Futurist Moment: Avant-garde, avant-guerre and the language of rupture*, Chicago, University of Chicago Press.

Pfaelzer, J. (1988) 'The changing of the avant-garde: The feminist utopia', *Science Fiction Studies*, 15, Part 3, 282–94.

Pfeil, F. (1988) 'Postmodernism as a "structure of feeling"', in C. Nelson and L Grossberg (eds) *Marxism and the Interpretation of Culture*, London, Macmillan, 381–403.

Pfeil, F. (1990) *Another Tale to Tell: Politics and narrative in postmodern culture*, London, Verso.

Piercy, M. (1979) *Woman on the Edge of Time*, London, The Women's Press.

Piercy, M. (1992) *Body of Glass*, London, Michael Joseph. First published as *He, She and It*, New York, Fawcett Crest (1991).

Porush, D. (1985) *The Soft Machine: Cybernetic Fiction*, New York and London, Methuen.

Poster, M. (1988) *Jean Baudrillard: Selected writings*, Cambridge, Polity Press/Basil Blackwell.

Probyn, E. (1987) 'Bodies and anti-bodies: Feminism and the postmodern', *Cultural Studies*, 1, Part 3, 349–60.

Radford, J. (ed.) (1986) *The Progress of Romance: The politics of popular fiction*, London and New York, Routledge and Kegan Paul.

Roberts, R. (1990) 'Postmodernism and feminist science fiction', *Science Fiction Studies*, 17, Part 2, 136–51.

Rorty, R. (1985) 'Habermas and Lyotard on postmodernity', in R. Bernstein (ed.) *Habermas and Modernity*, Cambridge, MA, MIT Press, 161–76.

Rose, J. (1986) *Sexuality in the Field of Vision*, London, Verso.

Rose, J. (1989) '*The Man who Mistook his Wife for a Hat* or *A Wife is Like an Umbrella* – fantasies of the modern and the postmodern', in A. Ross (ed.) *Universal Abandon? The politics of postmodernism*, Edinburgh, Edinburgh University Press, 237–50.

Rose, M.A. (1991) *The Postmodern and the Postindustrial*, Cambridge, Cambridge University Press.

Rosenthal, P. (1991) 'Jacked-in: Fordism, cyberpunk, Marxism', *Socialist Review*, Spring, 79–103.

Rosinsky, N. (1984) *Feminist Futures: Contemporary women's speculative fiction*, Michigan, UMI Research Press.

Ross, A. (ed.) (1989) *Universal Abandon? The politics of postmodernism*, Edinburgh, University of Edinburgh Press.

Ross, A. (1991) *Strange Weather: Culture, science, and technology in the age of limits*, London, Verso.

Rother, J. (1976) 'Parafiction: The adjacent universes of Barth, Barthelme, Pynchon, and Nabokov', *Boundary 2*, 5, 21–43.

Russ, J. (1972) 'The image of women in science fiction', in S.K. Cornillon (ed.) *Images of Women in Fiction: Feminist perspectives*, Bowling Green, OH, Bowling Green University Popular Press, 79–94.

Russ, J. (1973) 'Speculations: The subjunctivity of science fiction', *Extrapolation*, 15, Part 1, 51–9.

Russ, J. (1975) *The Female Man*, New York, Bantam.

Russ, J. (1980) '*Amor vincit foeminam*: The battle of the sexes in science fiction', *Science Fiction Studies*, 7, 2–15.

Russ, J. (1981) 'Recent feminist utopias', in M.S. Barr (ed.) *Future Females: A critical anthology*, Bowling Green, OH, Bowling Green University Popular Press, 71–85.

Russ, J. (1983) *How to Suppress Women's Writing*, Austin, The University of Texas Press.

Rutherford, J. (ed.) (1990a) *Identity: Community, culture, difference*, London, Lawrence and Wishart.

Rutherford, J. (1990b) 'A place called home: Identity and the cultural politics of difference', in Rutherford (ed.) *Identity: Community, culture, difference*, 9–27.

Said, E. (1978) *Orientalism*, London, Routledge and Kegan Paul.

Said, E. (1983) *The World, the Text, the Critic*, London, Faber and Faber.

Said, E. (1993) *Culture and Imperialism*, London, Chatto and Windus.

Salvaggio, R. (1984) 'Octavia Butler and the black science fiction heroine', *Black American Literature Forum*, 18, No. 2, 78–81.

Salvaggio, R. (1986) 'Octavia Butler', in M. Barr, R. Salvaggio and R. Law, *Suzy McKee Charnas, Octavia Butler, Joan D. Vinge*, Washington, Starmont House, 4–43.

Sargent, P. (ed.) (1978a) *Women of Wonder: Science fiction stories by women about women*, Harmondsworth, Penguin.

Sargent, P. (ed.) (1978b) *The New Women of Wonder: Recent science fiction stories by women about women*, New York, Vintage.

Sargent, P. (ed.) (1979) *More Women of Wonder: Science fiction novelettes by women about women*, Harmondsworth, Penguin.

Sargent, P. (1987) *The Shore of Women*, London, Chatto and Windus.

Scholes, R. (1975) *Structural Fabulation: An essay on the fiction of the future*, Notre Dame and London, University of Notre Dame Press.

Scholes, R. (1979) *Fabulation and Metafiction*, Urbana, University of Illinois Press.

Schulte-Sasse, J. (1987) 'Modernity and modernism, postmodernity and postmodernism: framing the issue', *Cultural Critique*, 5, 5–22.

Shepard, L. (1989) 'Waiting for the barbarians', *Journal Wired*, Part 1, 107–18.

Shiac, M. (1991) *Hélène Cixous: A politics of writing*, New York and London, Routledge.

Showalter, E. (ed.) (1981) *The New Feminist Criticism*, London, Virago.

Silliman, R., (1987) ' "Postmodernism": Sign for a struggle, the struggle for the sign', *Poetics Journal*, 7, 18–39.

Sim, S. (1992) *Beyond Aesthetics: Confrontations with poststructuralism and postmodernism*, Hemel Hempstead, Harvester Wheatsheaf.

Simone Maliqalim, T. (1989) *About Face: Race in postmodern America*, New York, Automedia.

Sloterdijk, P. (1984) 'Cynicism: The twilight of false consciousness', *New German Critique*, 33, 190–206.

Slusser, G. (1990) 'Literary MTV', in L. McCafferey (ed.) *Storming the Reality Studio*, Durham and London, Duke University Press, 334–42.

Sobchak, V. (1987) *Screening Space: The American science fiction film*, New York, Ungar.

Sobchak, V. (1988) 'Cities on the edge of time', *East–West Film Journal*, 3, Part 1, 4–17.

Sobchak, V. (1991) 'What in the world? New age mutant ninja hackers', *Artforum*, April, 24–6.

Sofia, Z. (1984) 'Exterminating fetuses: Abortion, disarmament, and the sexo-semiotics of extraterrestrialism', *Diacritics*, 14, no. 2, 47–59.

Spivak, G.C. (1990) *The Post-Colonial Critic: Interviews, strategies, dialogues*, ed. S. Harasym, New York and London, Routledge.

Springer, C. (1991) 'The pleasure of the interface', *Screen*, 32, no. 3, p. 303–23.

Staicar, T. (ed.) (1982) *The Feminine Eye: Science fiction and the women who write it*, New York, Frederick Ungar.

Stephanson, A., (1987) 'Regarding postmodernism – a conversation with Fredric Jameson', *Social Text*, 6, no. 2, pp. 29–54. Reprinted in A. Ross, (ed.) (1989) *Universal Abandon? The politics of postmodernism*, Edinburgh, University of Edinburgh Press, 3–30.

Sterling, B. (1986) *Schismatrix*, New York, Ace.

Sterling, B. (ed.) (1988) *Mirrorshades*, London, Paladin.

Sterling, B. (1989) *Islands in the Net*, London, Legend.

Sterling, B. (1990) *Crystal Express*, London, Legend.

Stratton, J. (1991) *Writing Sites: A genealogy of the postmodern world*, Hemel Hempstead, Harvester Wheatsheaf.

Suvin, D. (1979) *Metamorphoses of Science Fiction: On the poetics and history of a literary genre*, New Haven and London, Yale University Press.

Tasker, Y. (1991) 'Having it all: Feminism and the pleasures of the popular', in S. Franklin, C. Lury and J. Stacey (eds) *Off-Centre: Feminism and cultural studies*, London, HarperCollins Academic, 85–96.

Tatsumi, T. (1988) 'Some real mothers: An interview with Samuel R. Delany', *Science Fiction Eye*, 1, 5–11.

Tepper, S. (1989) *The Gate to Women's Country*, London, Bantam.

Tiptree, J. Jr. (1978) 'Houston, Houston, do you read?', in *Star Songs of an Old Primate*, New York, Ballantine, 164–226.

Trachtenberg, S. (ed.) (1985) *The Postmodern Moment*, Westport, CT, Greenwood Press.

Turner, B.S. (ed.) (1990) *Theories of Modernity and Postmodernity*, London, Sage.

Vonarburg, E. (1990) *The Silent City*, London, The Women's Press.

Walker, J. (1992) 'Cyberpunk', *Video Magazine*, 15 (January), 78.

Wall, C.A. (ed.) (1990) *Changing our own Words: Essays on criticism, theory, and writing by black women*, New York and London, Routledge.

Ward, A. (1987) 'Interview with Frederic [*sic*] Jameson', *Impulse*, 13, Part 4, 8–9.

Waugh, P. (1984) *Metafiction: The theory and practice of self-conscious fiction*, London and New York, Methuen.

Waugh, P. (1989) *Feminine Fictions: Revisiting the postmodern*, London and New York, Routledge.

Weedman, J.B. (ed.) (1985) *Women Worldwalkers: New dimensions of science fiction and fantasy*, Lubbock, TX, Texas Tech Press.

Weedon, C. (1987) *Feminist Practice and Poststructuralist Theory*, Oxford, Basil Blackwell.

Wellmer, A. (1985) 'On the dialectic of modernism and postmodernism', *Praxis International*, 4, 1, 337–62.

Whalen, T. (1992) 'The future of a commodity: Notes toward a critique of cyberpunk and the information age', *Science Fiction Studies*, 19, Part 1, 75–88.

White, H. (1986) 'Historical pluralism', *Critical Inquiry*, 12, Part 3, 480–93.

Wilcox, H., K. McWatters, A. Thompson and L. R. Williams (eds) (1990) *The Body and the Text: Hélène Cixous, reading and teaching*, Hemel Hempstead, Harvester Wheatsheaf.

Wilde, A. (1981) *Horizons of Assent: Modernism, postmodernism and the ironic imagination*, Baltimore and London, Johns Hopkins University Press.

Wilgus, N. (1978–9) '*Algol* interview: Suzy McKee Charnas', *Algol*, Winter, 21–5.

Wittig, M. (1979) *Les Guerilleres*, trans. D. Le Vay, London, The Women's Press.

Wittig, M. (1992) *The Straight Mind and Other Essays*, Hemel Hempstead, Harvester Wheatsheaf.

Wolin, R. (1984–5) 'Modernism vs postmodernism', *Telos*, 62, 9–29.

Wolmark, J. (1988) 'Alternative futures? Science fiction and feminism', *Cultural Studies*, 2, no. 1, 47–56.

Wolmark, J. (1990) 'The destabilisation of gender in Vonda McIntyre's *Superluminal*', in R. Garnett and R.J. Ellis (eds) *Science Fiction Roots and Branches: Contemporary critical approaches*, London, Macmillan, 168–82.

Wood, S. (1978–9) 'Women and science fiction', *Algol*, Winter, 9–18.

Woodward, K. (ed.) (1980) *The Myths of Information*, Madison, Coda Press.

Wolff, J. (1990) *Feminine Sentences*, Cambridge, Polity Press/Basil Blackwell.

Zaki, H. (1990) 'Utopia, dystopia, and ideology in the science fiction of Octavia Butler', *Science Fiction Studies*, 17, Part 2, 239–51.

Zimmerman, B. (1986) 'Feminist fiction and the postmodern challenge', in L. McCaffery (ed.) *Postmodern Fiction: A bio-bibliographical guide*, Westport, CT, Greenwood Press, 175–88.

Index